Leo and Mina Fink

Leo and Mina Fink

For the Greater Good

Margaret Taft

MONASH
UNIVERSITY
PUBLISHING

Leo and Mina Fink: For the Greater Good

© Copyright 2022 Margaret Taft

Monash University Publishing
Matheson Library Annexe
40 Exhibition Walk
Monash University
Clayton, Victoria 3800, Australia
publishing.monash.edu/

Monash University Publishing brings to the world publications which advance the best traditions of humane and enlightened thought.

This book has been peer reviewed.

ISBN: 9781922464866 (paperback)
ISBN: 9781922464873 (pdf)
ISBN: 9781922464880 (epub)

Design: Les Thomas
Typesetting: Jo Mullins

Cover image: Leo and Mina Fink, courtesy of the Fink family.

A catalogue record for this book is available from the National Library of Australia.

CONTENTS

'Leaders lead because there is work to do, there are people in need, there is injustice to be fought, there is wrong to be righted, there are problems to be solved and challenges ahead. Leaders hear this as a call to light a candle instead of cursing the darkness.'

Rabbi Jonathan Sacks,
Chief Rabbi of the United Hebrew Congregations
of the Commonwealth from 1991 to 2013

ACKNOWLEDGEMENTS

Delving into the extraordinary lives of Leo and Mina Fink was a great privilege but it would not have been possible without the support and enthusiasm of the Fink family. I am greatly indebted to the descendants of Leo and Mina, for their faith in me and their willingness to back this project. The three-year grant from The Leo and Mina Fink Fund enabled me to spend the necessary time researching and writing their important story. The family also gave me unfettered access to the goldmine of photographs and documents in their private collection.

I spent many happy hours interviewing family members, all of whom provided personal insights, anecdotal family stories and reflections on the life and times of Leo and Mina. I would like to personally thank Leo and Mina's children Freda Freiberg and the late Nathan Fink, Leo's nephews Barry Fink and Leon Fink, and grandson-in-law Colin Golvan, for welcoming me into their homes, and so generously giving me their time and their stories. Debbie Golvan, Lily Tell and Michael Fink, grandchildren of Leo and Mina, were always happy to answer my queries and provide additional information. Great grandson Raphael Tell enthusiastically provided input with my initial investigations.

A number of institutions were extremely helpful and willing to grant me permission to access their extensive archives. I spent many hours at the University of Melbourne examining the collection known as The Fink Papers, photographing documents and correspondence. Stephen Thomas, Jewish Care's General Manager in early 2019, generously provided a desk in his office and boxes of files that I could peruse and copy at leisure. The National Council of Jewish Women

(NCJW) opened its doors to me and allowed me to make copies of board minutes and past Bulletins. A big thank you to Lee Ann Basser, past CEO of NCJW for her support and who also invited me to give the annual Mina Fink lecture in 2019. It was a great honour to do so. The Holocaust Museum's co-President Sue Hampel eagerly introduced me to senior archivist Dr Anna Hirsh who welcomed me into the museum's archives and kindly provided me with past board minutes, newsletters and photos. I thank all these institutions and the wonderful individuals working in them for the positivity with which they embraced the project and their confirmation of the importance of telling Leo and Mina's story.

I thank my colleagues at the Australian Centre for Jewish Civilisation at Monash University for their support and encouragement at the project's inception, for their advice, guidance and scholarship. In particular I would like to thank Emeritus Professor Andrew Markus for his steadfast support of the entire project, Adjunct Professor Susannah Radstone for her advice in crafting the scope of the project and its initial proposal, Dr Daniel Heller for sharing his expertise on the education of Jewish women in interwar Poland and Dr Nathan Wolski for enthusing me with his passion for all things to do with Bialystok.

My sincerest thanks to the team at Monash University Publishing for supporting this publication and their belief in the power of the Fink story.

Photographs are reproduced with permission of individuals or holding institutions. Permission was also obtained to include excerpts of interviews. The views expressed in this book are my own. I have selected what I believe to be the most salient aspects of Leo and Mina's lives, those which best represent the fullness of their lives, their accomplishments and achievements, their hardships and the challenges they faced. I do not expect that everyone will agree with my selection or interpretation of events, the historical references I chose or my contextualisation. I do hope though that this dual biography will enrich the discourse of Australian Jewish history by highlighting the significant role played by exceptional individuals in shaping that history.

Lastly and most importantly I want to thank the two individuals who are central to this book, Leo and Mina Fink, who selflessly devoted their lives to building a better, fairer world and who did so with unflinching courage and compassion. In this they showed us all how best to live.

PREFACE

As a Melbourne-born child of post-war Jewish immigrants, I grew up knowing the name 'Fink'. Not personally, more as a brand, one that was synonymous with largess and good deeds. In their day, Leo and Mina Fink lived full, public lives. The Finks were the closest thing to Jewish royalty that I can remember. But I knew little else.

Today, one can hardly venture far in the Jewish community without stumbling upon the name Fink – brass plaques on buildings, educational programs, philanthropic endowments all named in their honour. But as is often the case, the history behind the plaques, the stories that underpin the endowments have become obscured over time. Lost from view. Forgotten. All that is left is the name. In this case 'Fink'.

Through the course of my recent research into the lives of immigrant Yiddish speakers in Melbourne, I kept seeing that name in a different context. No longer just an edifice or endowment, they again became flesh and blood individuals. At every turn, at the most critical junctures in the Jewish life of the city, I kept bumping into Leo and Mina Fink. There they were. Lives writ large. It piqued my interest. I wanted to know more.

The first challenge was to establish the facts, the biographical details surrounding these two public figures. The Fink family generously gave me access to boxes full of photographs, certificates, documents and letters. Interviews with family members complemented the written word with anecdotal evidence. But anecdotes are just that. Colourful, important stories that enhance and enrich, they add texture to dry hard facts, but they also require corroboration. Memory and the historical record don't always neatly align, but it can direct you towards important areas of investigation and discovery.

Archives in a number of different institutions provided another source of documentation. Archives are crucial source material but often present as a jumble of records lacking order, lacking context, lacking a timeline. I had boxes of precious papers that were, in their time, the ephemera of two peoples' lives, in random order without structure or cohesion. The eclectic nature of archival collections also renders many of them incomplete. These were no exception. Gaps emerged. Not everything was known. Not everything could be uncovered. But enough was there. Leo and Mina's lives were beginning to be fleshed out; what they did, when they did it, who they helped, the organisations they led, the social reforms they championed. Documents were put into sequential order, a time line emerged and a detailed chronology was constructed, all of which illuminated Leo and Mina's formidable life trajectory. Their story started to take shape.

Leo and Mina Fink were Jewish immigrants from Bialystok, Poland, who arrived in Melbourne in the interwar period. Leo arrived first, in 1928, the eldest of four brothers and a sister. The Fink family presented a typical rags-to-riches story; poor immigrants who came with nothing and became successful in business, were generous benefactors and were known to have an open door to many requests for assistance. Mina joined Leo as his wife in 1932. They lived comfortable affluent lives. They could have chosen to sit back, enjoy a life of ease and do little else. But they didn't.

In the mid-20th century, Leo and Mina Fink stood at the vanguard of sweeping changes to Melbourne's established Jewish community, a community that could trace its roots back to the First Fleet, but now increasingly under the influence of a highly visible, distinctive, newly arrived Yiddish-speaking Eastern European Jewish immigrant cohort. Leo and Mina quickly rose to play significant leadership roles as agents of change. By bringing the values, character and dynamism of an expansive, interconnected Eastern European Jewish world to Melbourne, they strengthened and transformed the nature and focus of the community. They helped to revitalise a moribund, highly assimilated community under the control of a conservative Anglocentric ruling elite into a powerful, proactive, outwardly focused network of democratically run organisations committed to the Jewish world and Jewish survival.

It is unusual to have a married couple in such close lock step with each other, sharing communal roles and encouraging and supporting each other in separate endeavours as Leo and Mina did. Together they undertook leadership roles that were transformative: in Jewish welfare, post-war Jewish immigration and the resettlement of thousands of Holocaust survivors. Together they lived a life dedicated to the service of others less fortunate. Later in life they forged separate leadership pathways, Leo pursuing his Zionist dream in Israel, Mina in women's affairs and Holocaust education and commemoration. Their actions were always prompted by the greater good, driven by the needs of the Jewish world.

Once the facts of their lives were laid bare, there was a far more compelling question that remained unanswered; 'why did they take it all on?' The answer to that question lies at the heart of this book, it drives the narrative. To understand 'why' they relentlessly pursued a life of communal service, the facts surrounding their lives had to be placed within their historical context. Nothing exists or happens in a vacuum. People's actions and deeds are not only dictated by the circumstances in which they find themselves but are shaped by their past and present lived experiences. The reasons underscoring the course they set themselves often lie buried in their early, formative years and the times in which they lived. Understanding these years was important in coming to grips with Leo and Mina's extraordinary story. So, this is also a story of those events and forces that influenced them; the perilous world in which they were born, the cataclysmic events they lived through, the Jewish world to which they were so deeply connected and the Australian world in which they lived, a new world that was liberating and empowering – all paint a full, vibrant picture while building the historical framework that helps us understand what motivated two individuals to live their lives so selflessly, so fearlessly in the service of others.

Leo and Mina's story is one that continues to resonate. At a time of heightened international turmoil, a war waged against a once in a life time pandemic, the threat of rising extremism and popularist politics, xenophobic fears over refugees and the impact of high immigration, the story of the Finks speaks to the power of individuals who, against all the odds, are able to invoke substantive and sustainable change on a global scale. Game changers. This is the story of how and more importantly why two immigrants took it upon themselves to save an entire world. Now that I know that about the Finks, perhaps it is time we all did.

Margaret Taft
2021

Chapter 1

AGAINST THE ODDS

'Daddy, daddy, it's me. Don't you recognise me?' A man with tears in his eyes stared unbelievingly at the grown girl crying out to him as she ran beside the boat.[1] 'It's me, Margot', she shouted at the father she had not seen for ten years.[2] The heartfelt reunion of this small fractured family, a Holocaust survivor and his daughter, was one of many that occurred on that hot Sunday afternoon, 16 March 1947.

Waiting at the wharf since the early hours of the morning were over 2000 members of Australia's Jewish community, eager to catch the first glimpse of the boat as it made its way through the choppy waters of Sydney harbour. Dozens of small craft crowded with relatives and friends circled the ship. Within a few short hours, 702 Jewish refugees, remnants of a Jewish world obliterated by war, stood on Australian soil.[3]

Scenes at the wharf made headline news. Emotions spilled over as the new arrivals made their way on shore. Men and women sobbed uncontrollably. Many stumbled over luggage as they rushed to reach a familiar face in the crowd.[4] Families embraced, falling into each other's arms. Friends were reunited, clutching each other for the first time since their lives were turned inside out. Some stood alone, quietly and patiently, stunned in disbelief. 'Were they really finally here?' Strangers, volunteers from the Australian Jewish Welfare and Relief Society spoke to them in Yiddish, Polish and German, gently explaining the arrival procedures to these newest Australians, as they were ushered through the customs shed and along the wharf.

There were 80 young children who arrived that day. Of these, 54 were between the age of three and 12; 26 were under the age of three.[5] Wide-eyed, they seemed to enjoy the heat of the day, taking in their new surroundings with little fuss, having grown accustomed to a constantly changing, transient existence. Some smiled at the strangers smiling at them. Some enjoyed being the centre of attention, unperturbed by the prying cameras, charged with capturing their momentous arrival for the daily newspapers.[6]

Fifteen-year-old refugee Frank Mohrer carried a crumpled, faded photograph of the father whom he had not seen for 12 years and could barely remember. Fred Mohrer fled Germany in 1935, leaving behind a wife who would be murdered by the Nazis and a young son. Fred found refuge in Melbourne, working as a manufacturer's agent. His son survived in an orphanage and later under guardianship in England where his father found him. Fred chartered a motor boat at 6am that morning to meet the ship as it steamed though the Heads. 'I'm sure he won't recognise me', he anxiously told a newspaper reporter.[7]

Many of the women were pregnant, several due to deliver that week.[8] New life in a new land. The oldest passenger was 82. Old life in a new land. More than half the adults were concentration camp survivors. Some bore the Auschwitz tattoo branded on their forearms, a constant reminder of a deeper wound that would never heal. One elderly man, a survivor of the hell that was Bergen Belsen, was seriously ill. Unable to disembark, he was helped off the ship and transferred to an ambulance. He would continue his journey to Melbourne by plane, where relatives would care for him.[9] Everywhere one could see the trauma of the past intrude on the present, as old worlds collided with the new. One woman screamed hysterically when a relative asked her to leave her baggage for later collection.[10] Was she momentarily taken back to that 'other world' where those who were ordered to discard their belongings were marked for certain, instant death?

They came from many different countries, the majority from Poland, others from the Netherlands, Germany, France and Austria, each with their own story of miraculous survival. But they all had one thing in common. Every Jewish refugee that arrived that day did so because their lives mattered. Not to a world worn down by the consequences of war, a world that had no interest in survivors of Nazi persecution, a world that wanted to move on and forget. But for a small band of Eastern European Jews who had spent the war years in the relative safety of Australia, and whose own lives intersected with a Jewish world that was no more, the lives of all survivors mattered deeply and could never be forgotten. Their resettlement in Australia became a rallying cry. Getting them here however, was another matter altogether. It would be the greatest challenge faced by this 'newcomer' community and those who rose to lead it, requiring a feat of human endeavour the likes of which had never been seen or undertaken in this strange new land.

When the Dutch ship that brought them, the *Johan de Witt*, docked that day at Pyrmont wharf no. 13, it did so amidst a storm of controversy. A decommissioned troopship hastily refitted to carry a very different kind of human cargo; the *Johan de Witt* only brought 72 passengers who were not Jewish. This meant that it contravened the Australian Government quota, in force since mid-1946, that limited the number of Jewish immigrants on any one vessel to 25 per cent. Only two boats ever got away with breaking the quota. The other, the *Hwa Lien* from Shanghai, docked in Sydney on 28 January 1947, and carried

306 Jewish refugees out of a total 474 passengers.[11] Arthur Calwell, the minister for immigration in the Chifley government grudgingly gave his approval. What followed was a public relations nightmare for the minister and his department. The press had a field day, labelling the *Hwa Lien*'s Jewish immigrants 'professional troublemakers', 'racketeers' and peddlers of false documents.[12] They were also accused of bribing officials and trickery. In allowing the *Hwa Lien* to dock, Calwell was accused of flooding the country with undesirable Jews. The arrival of the *Johan de Witt* two months later with twice the number of Jews and half the number of non-Jews was a breach too far. Calwell was furious with the one man he held personally responsible for flouting the quota, Leo Fink.

Polish born, pre-war Jewish immigrant Leo Fink was no stranger to controversy. During the darkest days of the Second World War, he seized control of Jewish welfare operations in Melbourne. Within two years he reconstituted the Australian Jewish Welfare and Relief Society into the most powerful Jewish organisation in the country, redirecting its focus from charitable domestic issues to one that fought to save a shattered Jewish world. Together with his young wife, the energetic and formidable Mina, a fellow Jewish immigrant, they were responsible for spearheading the rescue, relief and resettlement of thousands of Holocaust survivors in Australia. Between 1946 and 1955, 17,300 Jewish refugees would call Australia home.[13]

Leo and Mina Fink were part of a particular generation of Jewish immigrants who arrived in Australia in the decades prior to the outbreak of the Second World War. Both quickly rose to prominence. Their lives exemplified the intersection point that straddled the old world and the new. The old Jewish world of Eastern Europe, its distinctive way of life, its culture and language, its dependency on self-help and personal agency as a means of group survival and the opportunities and advantages that could be seized upon in a new, open and relatively free world.

Leo Fink and Arthur Calwell knew each other well. They had a good working relationship. Calwell would jokingly refer to Leo as the 'Jewish Minister for Immigration'. Knowing that Leo personally sponsored countless Jewish immigrants, acting as guarantor and mentor, Calwell was known to facetiously remark that 'he never knew a man who had so many cousins', to which Leo would respond 'that was because all Jews are related'.[14]

Both Leo and Mina would become known for their strong leadership. Both worked hard to build the sort of organisations that could execute the most complicated and ambitious plans. Both were great team builders. They knew that in order for their most audacious plan to succeed, the rescue and resettlement of Holocaust survivors, they also needed to have influence with the right people. It was a survival skill honed in the old world but equally applicable in the new. Leo skilfully forged strong connections with government officials, bureaucrats and departments. As a result, he had been able to call on Calwell's assistance on many occasions. But the arrival of the *Johan de Witt* was not one of them.

The *Johan de Witt* affair was some months in the making. In late December 1946 Leo took a frantic call from Lewis Neikrug, the Paris-based director general of the Hebrew Immigrant Aid Society (HIAS). 'Leo, I have the opportunity to send 700 Jews on the *Johan de Witt*. Get Calwell's OK. Do your utmost, it's very urgent, hundreds of people are on my doorstep.' Leo knew what Neikrug was referring to.[15]

In February 1946 Leo boarded one of the first commercial flights to leave Australia bound for Europe. His plan was to establish crucial ties with international Jewish relief agencies and secure urgent financial assistance, without which he could not undertake his bold plan to rescue survivors and resettle them in Australia.[16] Throughout his six-month trip he saw with his own eyes the plight of Jewish refugees desperate to leave behind a continent still infected with the scourge of antisemitism and crippled by the aftershocks of war. In Paris he encountered scores of destitute Holocaust survivors camped outside the HIAS office clutching landing permits to Australia but without the means of getting there. Leo, who had the good fortune to leave Europe for good in 1928, knew that he could easily have shared their fate – or worse.

In addition to the restrictive quota, the biggest problem facing postwar resettlement in Australia was the critical shortage of shipping. Landing permits could be obtained but without the means to transport them, the refugees remained unwanted inhabitants of overcrowded cities or languished in displaced persons camps. In either case they remained stateless refugees without hope of a better life. By 1947 a quarter of a million European Jews still remained displaced, unrepatriable.[17]

Throughout January 1947 the HIAS office cabled Leo who in turn communicated with Calwell regarding the capacity of the *Johan de Witt* and the percentage of Jews. The problem was that the number kept changing. What was anticipated as an acceptable percentage of Jews became a total. HIAS was unable to fill the boat it chartered with the mandatory 75 per cent fee-paying non-Jewish immigrants. It was a major obstacle for individuals like Leo and the Jewish agencies and would continue to plague rescue operations until the quota was lifted in February 1949, after considerable negotiations and handshake guarantees that the Jewish community would self-regulate the number of Jews it would sponsor into the country, never to exceed 3000 in any one year.[18]

By late January 1947 Calwell was notified that 'practically the whole of the [*Johan de Witt*] ship's accommodation will be taken up by Jewish migrants'. Leo approached Calwell but did not receive official approval to bring what would be the largest number of Jewish immigrants to ever enter Australia at one time. Responding to what Leo perceived as a state of emergency and in an act of brinkmanship, Leo gave Neikrug the go-ahead, gambling that the government would not turn the boat around. After all, the *Hwa Lien* made it through. These were immigrants with landing permits in hand, all had sponsors, were guaranteed accommodation and would not be a burden on the state. As legal immigrants they had a right to be here. Quotas were a tactical way of slowing down the rate of entry. Leo knew this. It was an audacious act, but Leo was never one to step away from a fight, especially when Jewish lives were at stake. Both Leo and Mina had learnt the bitter truth long ago, that Jews helping other Jews was the only way to survive. Leo would deal with any repercussions. Desperate times called for desperate means.[19]

Leo withstood the admonishment of Calwell who, incensed at what he felt was a deliberate act of sabotage, wrote to Leo on 27 January 1947, 'unless you [Leo] can … ensure that representations by you … are based on reliable data, I will have to protect my Department by having whatever information I receive from you carefully checked from official sources, notwithstanding that this may sometimes result … in the exclusion of your people from particular ships'. But Leo would not be swayed. As a successful businessman, he knew all about taking calculated risks.[20]

Not only did Leo have to contend with an enraged minister for immigration but his actions also jeopardised what was already a fraught relationship with the Sydney-based president of the Executive Council of Australian Jewry (ECAJ), Saul Symonds, who considered himself the rightful spokesman for Australian Jewry. Symonds rebuked Leo for overstepping the mark and usurping his authority. On 31 January 1947, Symonds wrote, 'With reference to the matter of the *Johan de Witt* ... in all matters of liaison between the Jewish community and the Minister, the liaison is between himself and myself.' Again, on 12 February 1947, Symonds reinforced his demand, 'Once again I would remind you that all official approaches on questions of refugees should be channelled through myself as liaison with the Minister'. In a further act of disunity, Symonds informed Calwell that Fink was acting as an individual and not as a representative of the Jewish community.[21] Leo's response to Symonds was predictably swift and furious. Most significantly it highlighted the stark cultural difference and leadership styles between Melbourne's growing Eastern European Jewish community of which Leo and Mina were rapidly becoming leading figures and Sydney's conservative 'establishment' Jews. It also revealed a great deal about Leo Fink the man, what he stood for and where his priorities lay. All of which were shared by his wife and confidante Mina.

> One cannot help noticing that the President of the ECAJ is not so much concerned with the real needs of Jewish immigration into this country as with the prestige and power of his own personality ... Are we bitterly concerned with Jewish immigration even to the extent of a little discomfort and even abuse to ourselves or are we just doing it in the cold matter of fact official way? ... The Relief Fund is out to help, assist and subsidize Jewish immigration into this country. It is prepared to look after the Welfare of new arrivals and it certainly expects to be consulted on matters of policy ... It is again this old NSW superiority complex, an attempt to wrest from Victoria and the leadership in today's crucial times when Jewish immigration is most vital for a Jewish future. On today's

immigration depends the survival of Jewish Communal life in this country. We can replenish and revitalise our stock today. It will be too late tomorrow ... We have no right to desert our brethren in their time of need. We have the right type of people here in Victoria who are prepared to bleed for their kith and kin ... We lack this mentality of my Jew and your Jew, Victorian Jew and NSW Jew, HIAS Jew and JOINT Jew ...[22]

The difficulties surrounding the arrival of Jewish immigrants was only part of the story. The task then turned to their rehabilitation and integration into the community. As subsequent chapters will reveal, it was in domestic matters rather than issues arising from immigration policy that Mina Fink's role in the resettlement of survivors came to the fore. As president of Jewish Welfare's influential Ladies' Group, she would lead her volunteer 'army', her female foot soldiers, a tireless team of some 900 co-workers, to undertake a range of duties. She recalled in a newspaper article late in life how no task was ever left to chance. They met newcomers at the wharves, packed meals for transit passengers, set up and managed migrant hostels, and provided comprehensive services covering language, accommodation, employment, childcare, health and business loans.[23]

It was a task that would stretch well into the 1950s with each successive wave of Jewish arrivals, from Hungary in 1956 and Poland in 1958. Even though professional social workers would increasingly replace the work of the volunteers throughout the 1950s, the commitment to the most vulnerable members of their community was one from which the Finks never shirked. Mina's own childhood trauma, being orphaned at the age of eight, instinctively directed her focus to the child survivors and the children of survivors. Her lifelong devotion to a group of orphans, the 'Buchenwald Boys' began with their arrival in the late 1940s and continued until her death in 1990. This was more than a moral obligation to help those in need. This was repairing and replenishing a Jewish world of which Leo and Mina were very much a part.

Rumblings about the excessive number of Jews arriving on the *Johan de Witt* began appearing in the press in February, once news of its departure from Marseille was made public. From as far away as Kalgoorlie in Western Australia to Sydney and Melbourne, alarmist articles warned about the impending invasion of Jews. 'Many Migrants, But None British' Melbourne's *The Age* complained on 12 February 1947, also warning of an imminent 'Influx of Jews'. *The Kalgoorlie Miner* echoed the sentiment on 13 February 1947 – '600 Jews for Australia'. Not wanting to be caught on the back foot again, Calwell justified the lack of suitable British passengers by claiming that conditions on the boat were 'unsuitable for British migrants … accommodation on the *Johan de Witt* consists of hammocks and stand-ups in the holds, and will be very rough'.[24] Calwell was right. The state of all these migrant ships was deplorable. Mina Fink remembered them as 'rotten old hulks, former troop ships on their last legs'.[25] Calwell also explained that the *Johan de Witt* was 'not under charter to the Commonwealth government'.[26] Right again, the boat was hired and paid for by two Jewish international philanthropic organisations, Hebrew Immigrant Aid Society (HIAS) and the American Jewish Joint Distribution Committee (the Joint). The Australian Government never made any financial investment in Jewish immigration. Great effort was made to defuse the situation, with Calwell also confirming that the 'landing permits were issued over a year ago by close relatives who were able to guarantee maintenance and accommodation of their nominees'.[27] So why the fuss?

While Australia had embarked on an ambitious post-war nation building exercise with an expansive immigration program as its cornerstone, Jewish refugees were not the type of immigrant the government had in mind. Nor the general public. Non-Jewish immigrants felt the same way. On the *Johan de Witt* a British chemist travelling on to New Zealand with his wife and infant son declared, 'I would not have taken passage had I known I was to travel with the [Jewish] migrants'.[28] Australia preferred British immigrants but favourable publicity was also given to Calwell's Northern European 'Blond Balts', boat loads of fair-skinned, fair-haired immigrants who looked the part and would easily blend in. In March 1947 a gallup poll reported that 58 per cent of respondents were against the resettlement of Jewish refugees in Australia.[29] In another poll undertaken in 1948, 60 per cent wanted to keep Jews out. It found 25 per cent only wanted to let a few in.[30] The voting public was not on side. Perhaps that explains the government's desire to keep Jewish immigration to an inconspicuous trickle rather than a flood.

The government need not have worried about an uncontrolled influx of Jews. It made sure it had a raft of measures in place to monitor and restrict the number of Jews entering the country, only repealing them once the majority of Jewish refugees in Europe had been resettled. The contentious 'Are you Jewish?' question on all Form 40 applications for those sponsored by relatives and Form 47 for those sponsored by the Australian Jewish Welfare and Relief Society, remained in place until 1953. The Iron Curtain Embargo, under the guise of security concerns, prohibited immigrant entry from all communist countries from October 1949 until 1954. Australia's agreement with the International Refugee Organization (IRO) to accept European migrants and provide assisted travel, initially excluded Jews as well as a number of nationalities.

Even when restrictions were lifted, only a small number, some 250 Jews out of 180,000 arrived on the IRO scheme. In the decade 1945 to 1955 Australia admitted nearly one million 'New Australians', only 1.8 per cent were Jews.[31]

Leo and Mina knew they were swimming against the tide of popular public opinion and government policy by advocating for and assisting with Jewish immigration. Not wanting to exacerbate what was already a volatile situation, they ensured that the disembarkation of the *Johan de Witt* was well organised, executed with military precision. A team of thirty volunteers from the Australian Jewish Welfare and Relief Society, led by Melbourne-based welfare stalwart, former Warsaw immigrant David Abzac and Sydney's Syd Einfeld, had been dispatched to ensure that every aspect of the arrival procedure was carried out in an orderly manner. As a result of a wharf labourers' strike, the passengers assisted the volunteers with bringing their own luggage on shore. The 'new arrivals' were guided through and assisted with customs, fed freshly cut sandwiches while the children were given ice cream and lemonade, all of which was set out on white clothed trestle tables and served by a small team of women, before being ferried onto their next destinations, 400 of whom would travel by train to Melbourne for permanent resettlement.[32] They were encouraged not to linger on the wharf and not to talk to strangers. Little English was spoken.[33]

It was the only voyage the *Johan de Witt* made to Australia in peacetime but it cemented its place in history.[34] While 71 ships and 32 airplanes carrying Jewish immigrants – displaced persons from Europe and Shanghai – arrived in those early, chaotic post-war years, it was the *Johan de Witt*, with its burgeoning immigrant cargo that epitomised the desperate struggle between individuals such as Leo and Mina Fink, the organisations they led and the many forces that obstructed their rescue mission.[35] They battled shipping shortages, manoeuvred their way around restrictive and discriminatory government policies, placated government ministers and bureaucrats, challenged leaders within their own community and stood firm against the powerful sway of public opinion and government obfuscation – in order to bring their fellow Jews to these shores. While Jews were but a small percentage of Australia's overall immigration intake, it nevertheless doubled the size of Australian Jewry within one decade. Once here Jewish Welfare and private sponsors took full responsibility for their resettlement, their integration and their welfare. It was a herculean effort that required ingenuity and 'know how', prodigious local fundraising and unparalleled assistance from international Jewish agencies, all of which was unmatched in the history of Australian post-war immigration. Above all it required the courage of conviction.

The young reporter who captured the historic arrival of the *Johan de Witt* for the *Sydney Jewish News* was a 19-year-old German Jewish refugee, Eugene Kamenka, who had arrived in Australia in 1937 and who would go on to make his mark as a professor of political philosophy and Marxism. The scene at the wharf had a profound effect on him. Unlike the non-Jewish press which more often than not was keen to report on smuggled contraband, the filthy onboard conditions, the lack of sanitation, the cacophony of foreign languages rather than the mellifluous sound of the King's English, Kamenka was witness to something very different that Sunday afternoon.

As they filed down the ship's gangway, Kamenka saw battle scarred survivors of an horrific war that had spawned a new word, 'genocide'. Most had been inmates of notorious concentration camps, others survived in hiding, often in mortal fear of being discovered or betrayed and executed. Some were able to escape to the relative safety of neutral or unoccupied countries only to be declared 'enemy aliens' who then faced internment. A renowned resistance fighter, a survivor of the Warsaw ghetto uprising who bravely took on the might of the Third Reich in a doomed, yet heroic act of defiance, also disembarked with his young wife that day. Everywhere he looked Kamenka saw the remnants of a lost world. He made mention that many were professionals, such as Hans Zander who had been the assistant director of the Berlin State Opera. Zander escaped to England in 1939. During the war years he was connected with the Entertainment National Service Association (ENSA) units. There were lawyers, doctors, as well as merchants, tailors and labourers. These were not the 'refuse of Europe' as the president of the Australian Natives' Association (ANA) PJ Lynch told the Melbourne *Sun* two days after the *Johan de Witt*'s arrival, nor the 'inferior stock' referred to by Ken Bolton, president of the NSW Returned Servicemen's League.[36] These were, as Kamenka depicted them, men, women and children desperate for a chance at life.

Leo and Mina Fink did not know the young girl or the father with whom she was reunited on that fateful day in March 1947. Indeed, it is unknown if they personally knew any of the 'newcomers' on the *Johan de Witt*. While they were present when many new arrivals stepped ashore, they were not there when the *Johan de Witt* docked. They didn't have to be. For Leo and Mina Fink these survivors were part of the larger Jewish family that united them all. This was about restoring the heart and soul of a broken Jewish world, their world, their family. 'All Jews are related' wasn't just a flippant retort Leo made to appease Calwell, but testament to the human chain that linked Leo and Mina to Jewish humanity. They knew that by helping individuals rehabilitate their own lives they were rebuilding and reviving a Jewish world torn apart. And while that world no longer had a home on the

European continent it would be strengthened and thrive within a new community in a new land under the Southern Cross.

The rescue and resettlement of Holocaust survivors would come to define Leo and Mina Fink, but it was not the beginning nor the end of their story. Leo and Mina were on the frontline of some of the most significant cultural and social changes to overtake Australia's Jewish community in the 20th century. They were transformative leaders, fearless and tenacious, yet compassionate and empathetic, who lived their lives in the service of others.

So, what made these two ordinary individuals become the heroes of such an extraordinary tale? Let us rewind to a very different time and place. Let us try to understand what shaped and defined two people who would take on the world in order to save a world.

Chapter 2

THERE'S SOMETHING ABOUT BIALYSTOK

It all began in a place called Bialystok. Situated 180km east of Warsaw, Bialystok sat on the crossroad of the Russian empire and the Polish nation, a bustling, burgeoning border town, located in a heavily forest-ed region that divided Poland from Belorussia and Lithuania. Leo and Mina spent their formative years there, in the early part of the 20th century. Both experienced life in this volatile, vibrant metropolis during a particularly tumultuous period in the history of Eastern European Jewry. It was a time and place that would come to shape Leo and Mina's world view, strengthen their Jewish consciousness and identity, deepen their connection to the Jewish world, expose them to the trauma of a life lived in extremely challenging times and instil in them resilience and adaptability. Above all, it shone a light on the pathway towards Jewish continuity. It taught them how to survive.

'I am a product of the shtetl', Leo reminisced late in life, referring to the Yiddish word meaning a small town or village.[1] Leo referred to himself and Mina as 'shtetl' Jews, invoking a romanticised yet inaccurate view of what their life had really been like. Forget *Fiddler on the Roof.* This was no 'Anatevka'. Bialystok was no bit player on the large stage of Polish Jewish urban life. To portray Bialystok as a small, parochial town diminishes its significance and underplays its unique character. This was no ordinary backwater 'shtetl' and Leo and Mina were no ordinary small minded 'shtetl' Jews. Bialystok proved just how complicated and multifaceted the Polish Jewish experience was.

What set Bialystok apart from other emerging industrial cities in Eastern Europe, all with large Jewish populations, was the nature of its Jewishness. At the turn of the 20th century Bialystok had a Jewish population close to 48,000. Although more Jews lived in cities such as Warsaw and Lodz, Bialystok's Jewish population constituted 75 per cent of its total inhabitants, making it a city with one of the densest Jewish populations in Europe at that time. A significant factor in shaping Bialystok's distinctive character, its strong Jewish majority helped to transform the city into a Jewish space by creating a unique environment in which Jewish culture flourished, Jewish identity was strengthened and indeed dominated.[2]

Bialystok represented the Jewish world in all its drama, a town that encapsulated all that was good and all that was bad. You could be forgiven for thinking that a city with such a high percentage of Jews would be safeguarded against the oldest hatred of all, but Bialystok was also a town plagued by antisemitism. Jewish life was an endless struggle. Jew hatred, sporadic pogroms, systemic discrimination, violence and destruction were commonplace. From the cradle to the grave, Bialystok offered its constituents life's entirety, everything the Jewish world had to offer and everything that threatened its existence. Bialystok had the lot. And Leo and Mina Fink spent the first 19 turbulent years of their lives in the thick of it all.

In the Beginning

By the latter part of the 19th century Bialystok had become the major transit stop for the railway between St Petersburg and Warsaw, a central depot which enabled the city's textile industry to flourish. Between

1867 and 1897 the number of textile mills increased from 89 to 309. By 1898 the Jews owned 80 per cent of the city's large mills; Jewish workers constituted 83.9 per cent of the work force in what were pre-mechanised factories. Jews also comprised 88 per cent of the city's shopkeepers.[3]

By the beginning of the 20th century nearly 100,000 Jews had migrated to and from the city in search of better prospects and greater prosperity.[4] The Finks were one such family, excited by the opportunities offered in a growing industrial metropolis. Mordechai and Masza Fink (née Jablonski) relocated from the small neighbouring town of Krynki, 45km east of Bialystok, shortly after the birth on 31 October 1901 of the first of their five children, Itzhak Leib, to be known as 'Leo'. Population movements like that brought more than economic opportunity. People brought ideas with them. It ensured that Jewish Bialystok was constantly exposed to changing political, social and cultural movements and injected with the ideals that accompanied them.[5]

Twelve years Leo's junior, Miriam 'Mina' Waks was born on 5 December 1913, the second of three children to Nathan and Freda Waks (née Kaplan). The Waks family were already residents of Bialystok by the late 19th century. Mina's grandfather Joseph Waks was a cloth weaver and part of the expanding textile industry. Her grandmother Sheina Sura Waks (née Surasky) was the daughter of a Hasidic rabbi of considerable standing and the family held on to orthodox traditions.[6] They were financially secure. By the time Mina was born, the Finks were also self-sufficient textile entrepreneurs. A licence of trading enterprise was granted to Mordechai Fink on 15 May 1913, for a business on Gogolevshaya Street, including the 'rental of mechanical motors'.[7]

Culture, Charity, Community

While Bialystokers often spoke Russian and Polish, the mother tongue was Yiddish. A rich language that became a cultural identity marker of Eastern European Jews, Yiddish was a language that belonged to a people but never to a country. A language that was not constrained by borders, it gave its speakers the gift of being part of a transnational, interconnected world.[8]

In Bialystok Yiddish was spoken in the home, heard on the streets, in the cafes and in the marketplace, in the factories and throughout the commercial sector. Yiddish developed its own body of literature, its own poetry and prose. Yiddish was taught as a living, breathing language in schools and was deeply woven into the fabric of everyday Jewish life. Leo and Mina were part of Bialystok's Yiddish-speaking, Yiddish-loving community. Yiddish life and its connection to the Jewish world would remain at the core of their existence.

Eastern European Yiddish-speaking communities spawned elaborate networks of community organisations and institutions that formed the bedrock of everyday life. Group survival depended on it. Bialystok had a flourishing independent press with four daily Yiddish newspapers, writers such as Pesach Kaplan who edited the newspapers *Unzer Lebn (Our Life)* and *Dos Naye Lebn (The New Life)*, authors such as short-story writer Aron Berezinski and the humourist Yisrael Sztajnsafir, and poets such as Mendl Goldman.[9]

Contemporary professional theatre companies such as the Bialystok Habima, established in 1912, performed to great acclaim, one of its rising stars was Israel Beker who would later become director of Tel Aviv's Habima Theatre. In his later years Beker was known to proudly proclaim, 'I am not just from Bialystok, I am a Bialystoker and that means much more'.[10] There were a number of amateur dramatic circles and theatrical societies. Artists found an appreciative audience for their work and the early figurative painter Benzion Rabinowicz would later move to Paris and collaborate with Marc Chagall in the post-war years.

A network of self-help charities began in 1879 when a committee was established to help needy Jews. There was no other way to survive. In 1905 it became the Jewish Charitable Society and by 1912 it had 1305 members. In 1882 an old-age home was established and in 1885 the *Linas Hatsedek* society was formed to give emergency aid to the sick. Educational institutions catered for the religious, the secular and the progressive, while sports associations that catered for all physical endeavours including athletics, football, cycling and gymnastics thrived. Between 1910 and 1914 an imposing new synagogue was built at an estimated cost of 50,000 rubles.[11]

Bialystok invested heavily in its social capital. Wherever they would venture in the world, Bialystokers became known as great leaders and institution builders. Melbourne would become one of four cities with a strong diasporic Bialystok community, one that set the benchmark for organisational development and social action. The other centres were Tel Aviv, New York and Buenos Aires. Being a Bialystoker in Melbourne held great currency.[12]

'What Was Best for the Jews?'

Bialystok was also a hotbed of revolutionary political activism. From the late 19th century after periods of economic recession, factory workers began to rebel against exploitative practices used by factory owners. The first major strike in Russian Jewish society took place in Bialystok in 1882 when 70 weavers abandoned their looms in protest over poor wages. Its success prompted other workers to employ strike action as a means of protest. By the beginning of the 20th century Jews swelled the ranks of dozens of illegal political organisations. Every illegal political group active in Imperial Russia had a thriving branch in Bialystok. There was an understanding that you had to fight for what was right and fight for what was fair.[13] In later life Leo became known as a tough negotiator, but a fair combatant. 'Fairness' was as equally important to Leo as winning.

Three major nationalist movements that stoked the fires of bitter confrontations and generated heated debates were well represented in Jewish Bialystok; Zionism, the Bund and Esperanto. Each offered different responses to the challenges of Jewish life in an increasingly dangerous world. Each believed it had the answers to the perennial question 'What was best for the Jews?'

Secular Zionism had its origins in the late 19th century when the word 'Zionism' was adopted to describe the Jewish nationalist movement in which *Eretz Yisrael* (the land of Israel) becomes a Jewish homeland. The father of political Zionism, Theodor Herzl was convinced that Jews could never be fully integrated into European life. For him Jewish emancipation was a myth and a Jewish homeland the only viable option.[14] In Bialystok there were Zionist groups of the political left, the right and the centre, each with their own agenda on the way to establish and govern a Jewish state, but all in agreement that a Jewish homeland was the only solution to the burning issue of Jewish survival in a hostile world.

Bialystok was also a stronghold of the socialist, secular Bund, a powerful organisation in the interwar years that advocated for the advancement of Jewish life in the towns in which Jews lived, opposing a Jewish homeland in *Eretz Yisrael*. In simple terms the Bund advocated for 'hereness' as opposed to Zionism which supported 'thereness'. Origins of the Bund go back to a meeting held in the home of a blacksmith in Vilna in 1897 consisting of 15 Jewish socialists who voted to form a new political movement, 'Der Algemener Yiddisher Arbeter Bund in Rusland un Poyln' (General Jewish Workers Union in Russia and Poland), to be known as the Bund, the Yiddish word for Union. Unlike Zionism, which supported modern Hebrew as the Jewish national language, the Bund clung to Yiddish as its national language. Yiddish remained a cornerstone of its cultural identity. The Bund soon became engaged in political agitation, workers strikes and Jewish self-defence. The Bund became known as defenders of the home front.[15]

Families could often be divided on issues of national identity and differing political allegiances. However, family loyalties would often trump ideological differences. Mina was raised in a staunch Zionist home and would remain a supporter of the State of Israel her entire life, as would Leo, but her uncle, Jacob Waks, her father's younger brother, was a firebrand leader of the Bund in Bialystok, leading workers in strike action and often landing himself in jail as a consequence. Her relationship with him would remain strong regardless of their political differences. She would come to save his life when the hell and fury of the Second World War threatened to take it. Jacob Waks and Leo would work closely together in matters pertaining to Jewish welfare and the Jewish community.

Bialystok was the birthplace of the Esperanto movement led by Bialystok-born Ludwik Zamenhof, a Polish Jewish ophthalmologist and intellectual, and the architect of 'The International Language', an invented, innovative language designed to promote ethnic understanding. Zamenhof and his supporters believed that a universal language would break down barriers and divisions within society and improve the chances of world peace. Zamenhof believed that his childhood experiences in Bialystok where he watched Jews, Russians, Poles, Ukrainians bait and taunt each other demonstrated the need for a common language. It failed because it simplistically assumed that language was the only divisive issue confronting different ethnic groups.[16] Zamenhof's first home in Zielona Street, also known in Yiddish as the *Yatke Gasse* or Butchers Street, was where the Fink family lived during the First World War, in the house directly opposite the birthplace of Ludwik Zamenhof.

Pogroms, Wars, Death and Disease

Leo was only five years old when he had his first taste of endemic Jew hatred. Bialystok experienced a devastating pogrom in the summer of 1906. Violence erupted on 1 June, continuing for two days, with more than 80 people murdered by soldiers of the Imperial Russian Army and *Chernoe Znamia* (The Black Banner) a Russian anarchist communist organisation. More than 100 Jews were injured, some reports say the figure was closer to 200, 169 shops and properties were torched and looted, and several streets completely destroyed. The pogrom was one of the most brutal expressions of antisemitic violence against Russian Jewry that year. The actions of Jewish self-defence groups helped to spare some of the working-class sections of the city, arguably saving hundreds if not thousands of lives.[17] The lesson was clear. Jews had to defend themselves. They had to fight their own battles. Self-defence and self-preservation were life lessons instilled in the young Leo. From then on, as Leo would recount later in life, he walked to school accompanied by an older cousin and always carried stones in his pocket, ready to defend himself against marauding gangs.

When Mina was six months old, on 28 June 1914, Archduke Franz Ferdinand of Austria was assassinated, catapulting the world into its first major global conflict, and quickly sweeping Bialystok into its orbit of death and destruction.[18] Bialystok found itself at the centre of heavy fighting. Swiftly brought under harsh German occupation in early 1915, the war devastated the local economy, uprooted thousands and spread famine and disease throughout the region. It decimated the local inhabitants. Many faced economic ruin and starvation. Bombardment destroyed the Jewish hospital, synagogues and schools that had been built by the early Jewish settlers in the late 19th century. The city's Jewish population plummeted, falling from 61,500 in 1913 to 37,186 in 1921.[19] The Fink and Waks families remained in the city, although the fallout of the Great War would leave its deadly mark on both families.

When the 'war to end all wars' came to its conclusion on 11 November 1918, the mood in Bialystok was neither peaceful nor celebratory. Bialystok's economy never fully recovered. The Russian market was lost in 1920, the newly installed Polish Government refused to re-invest in Bialystok's redevelopment and hyperinflation added to these difficulties. And yet the Jews of Bialystok withstood the hardships to continue life amidst the turmoil. The community sought to rebuild. And they were not left alone in their hour of need. Immediate support came from other Bialystoker living in the Diaspora. In New York in 1919 the 'Bialystoker Centre' was formed with a 'mission to coordinate relief efforts to rebuild Bialystok'.[20] Spiritual and financial aid came from a greater Bialystok that spanned the globe. The Fink and Waks families were part of a global community that were bound together by a common identity and a common sense of purpose. An international fraternity of *landsman*, a deeply interconnected Jewish world that would provide aid and assistance, set the template for the kind of outreach that Leo and Mina would come to undertake in another corner of the world, when Jewish survival faced its greatest threat.

Mina's maternal grandparents, the Kaplans, were particularly hard hit by the economic downturn, and although financially devastated, they maintained a way of life steeped in Jewish moral values.[21] There was some economic improvement though and the outlook was not entirely bleak. The Jewish community displayed its usual resilience. Many bounced back. By 1921 Jews ran 93 per cent of the city's businesses and owned 89 per cent of its factories. In 1923 Mordechai Fink's business prospects were improving, and he was listed as proprietor of a spinning mill on 40 Slominska Street, employing 24 workers.[22]

In addition to the economic woes brought on by the First World War, Eastern Europe remained locked in a deadly cycle of violence and destruction. Bialystok the border town, was again caught in the crossfire.

The Russian civil war, which began with the Bolshevik revolution in 1917 and lasted until 1922, incorporated the struggle for Ukrainian independence. The war consisted of a series of military conflicts between different political and military forces. Belligerents included Ukrainian nationalists, anarchists, Bolsheviks, the forces of Germany and Austria–Hungary, the White Russian Volunteer army, and the Second Polish Republic forces. The conflict wreaked havoc on many fronts, between Red (the military force of the communist Bolsheviks) and White (anti-communists led by former Imperial officers) Russian armies, between Ukrainians and Poles. In the absence of any central controlling authority, units within all participating armies attacked the Jews.[23] While there is no conclusive data which details the exact number of Jewish fatalities during the civil wars, evidence points to approximately 60,000 deaths and many times that of the wounded, while other accounts say the Jewish death toll was closer to 100,000.[24] Over the course of a few short years, Bialystok was governed by Czarist

Russia, occupied by the Germans and finally came under the control of the nationalist Poles as part of the Second Polish Republic established in 1919. Leo and Mina's families learnt to accommodate, to adapt and in spite of uncertainties, hardships and setbacks, they endured.

Tragedy Strikes

Disease and famine were every bit as deadly, if not more so. The typhus epidemic which spread across the Badlands of Eastern Europe from 1918 until 1922 claimed three million Russian and Polish lives. One of those fatalities was Mina's father Nathan Waks. Shortly after, Mina's mother, Freda Waks, committed suicide. As if the trauma of being orphaned wasn't enough, it was Mina who found her mother's lifeless body. From the age of eight, Mina was without parental support. But Mina was not entirely alone. Her maternal grandparents, Brajna (née Senderowicz) and Eliezer Kaplan gave her and her younger brother Jacob (Jack) a loving and secure home. In a time of turmoil, they gave Mina stability and security. Her older brother Lolek (Leo) went to live with their paternal Waks grandparents. In 1921 Lolek was sent to a religious boarding school in Germany, where he later completed an engineering degree. His diploma, complete with Nazi insignia, remains with the family to this day. By this time both the Waks grandparents had died. Though not wealthy, the Kaplans ensured Mina had a sound education and instilled in her a love of family and the importance of family support. Eliezer Kaplan, a proud Zionist, also imparted a love of the Zionist cause. Mina retained these values for the rest of her life.[25]

In 1920, tragedy befell Leo's family. His younger sister Zyna, a bright and scholarly girl, one year Leo's junior, contracted post-viral encephalitis following the influenza pandemic of 1918 and 1919, a particularly virulent influenza strain also called the 'Spanish flu'. This pandemic killed an estimated 50 million people worldwide, targeting not just the most vulnerable, the elderly and the very young, but those who would otherwise have been considered fit and healthy. Left permanently and severely disabled, Zyna was never institutionalised but cared for by her parents until her death in 1946 aged 44. Again, the strength of family prevailed.[26]

Mina was still a child in 1920, learning to adapt to a life without parents. Her family was split apart, her life changed forevermore. The 1920s is a decade conspicuous by the presence of absence for Mina. There are no photographs or documents that have survived of Mina during this period. No evidence of a private life lived in the shadow of tragedy. But we do know a great deal about what influenced her and what would remain a constant in her life; education.

A Network of Schools

At the end of the First World War the Jews of Poland established, developed and maintained a large network of different types of schools, each supported by various social and political organisations whose philosophies were imparted by the schools themselves. These 'modern' schools were seen as being instrumental in moulding the minds of the next generation of Jews. The Cysho schools (Central Yiddish School Organisation) were created by the Bund and Left Poale Zion, with Yiddish as the language of instruction. The Tarbut schools were established by the Zionist movement, with Hebrew as the medium of instruction. The bilingual schools were operated by the Federation of Societies for the Support of Jewish Schools, with either Hebrew-Polish or Hebrew-Yiddish as the language of instruction. The ultraorthodox Agudah schools – Horev for boys and Beis Yaacov for girls – with a knowledge of the Torah as the exclusive ideal of education and the orthodox Mizrachi schools aiming for an integration of the religious and national elements in Jewish life were established by the orthodox Jewish leaders.[27]

Jewish girls' education in the interwar period in Poland was liberating and empowering. Even those who attended the Beis Yaacov schools undertook secular subjects as it was a state requirement demanded by state educational authorities. Mina was not a student of Beis Yaacov. Her education was secular, far-reaching and cultivated a wide interest in language, literature, the natural sciences and the arts. In the final four years of Mina's secondary education, she attended the Druskin Gymnasium (high school), one of six co-educational high schools in Bialystok. The Druskin Gymnasium, located at 4 Szlacheckiej was a private, prestigious Jewish Gymnasium established in 1911 by the progressive educator Dawid Druskin. In 1919 Polish became the language of instruction, following the establishment of the Second Polish Republic, and in 1925 it offered its first Baccalaureate (matriculation). In 1926 the Druskin Gymnasium had 145 students. By the early 1930s, when Mina was in her final years, the student number had doubled, its reputation had spread and it was recognised as a leading educational provider by the Polish Government. Most importantly the Druskin Gymnasium exposed Mina to a world of possibilities, a world in which women held intellectual parity with men. The very nature of her education promoted female empowerment and personal agency. She graduated in 1932 with a broad range of subjects that included religious education, Polish language, Latin, French, history, geography, natural sciences, mathematics, art and physical education.[28] More importantly she emerged as a confident, resilient, self-assured young woman capable of adapting to a rapidly changing environment.[29]

In 1920 Leo graduated from a non-Jewish school, the Gymnasium of the First Bialystok Society of Teachers on 28 June 1920. The school, established in 1918, later became the prestigious Zeligman Gymnasium in 1922. The language of instruction was Russian (until 1921) then Polish. Leo was an excellent student, graduating with a second-class distinction. Subjects included Russian language and literature, Polish, German, French, Latin, mathematics, physics, geography, history, natural science, legal studies and philosophy.[30] Like other young Jewish boys, Leo's proficiency in the Yiddish language and his ability to read Hebrew scripture came from being taught outside of formal school hours in special religious schools called *Cheders*. Leo would remain a lifelong learner, a lover and collector of books and a supporter of those who wrote them. Later in life, Leo accumulated an impressive private library on a vast range of subjects.

Life's Lessons

Leo and Mina learnt about the harsh realities of life firsthand, but they also learnt about the strength that can come from within and the importance of self-reliance. With support from one's own community one can overcome what might seem insurmountable obstacles. Mina did not let tragedy break her. She learnt that what one needed was to maintain a connectedness to others. Strong family ties, sound social networks and a well-grounded education were empowering and enabling. A well-honed set of life skills would not only ensure their own survival, but, when called upon, those of an entire community.

Leo and Mina's experiences in Bialystok shaped the way they approached challenges in any corner of the world. They experienced wars, epidemics, antisemitism, encounters with nationalist politics and the collapse of an economy. They endured personal hardship and tragedy. They both benefited from a broad, progressive secular education while developing an understanding of the important role played by Jewish organisations to ensure Jewish survival. This underpinned their own transformation into modern, adaptable, free thinking, urban Jews. While Bialystok provided them with a world within a world, it also prepared them to fearlessly step out of that world and embrace the opportunities of another. While Leo and Mina would leave Bialystok for good, Bialystok would never leave them.

Chapter 3

BECOMING LEO

The year 1920 signalled the beginning of a new life for Leo. For the 19-year-old school graduate, it was the start of many adventures, a life filled with new experiences and new prospects. Leo would never live permanently in Bialystok again, only returning intermittently to visit family. Within a few short years Leo would become a citizen of the world. What was it that initially stirred his wanderlust? Was it, as one family member suggested, his desire to dodge possible conscription in a Polish army slogging it out in a war between the Second Polish Republic, the Ukrainian People's Republic and the Soviet Union, a war that incurred tens of thousands of casualties both military and civilian?[1] Or was there something even more immediate, more compelling and promising that fired his imagination?

A Pioneering Life

The Balfour Declaration, issued in a letter by Arthur James Balfour, the British foreign secretary, on 2 November 1917 to Lionel Walter Rothschild, the 2nd Baron Rothschild (of Tring) a leader of British Jewry, gave support for 'the establishment in Palestine of a national home for the Jewish people'. It gave hope and aspiration, but fell short of the expectations of Zionist leaders who had hoped for the reconstitution of Palestine as 'the' Jewish national home. The declaration was deliberately vague and non-committal, stipulating that 'nothing shall be done which may prejudice the civil and religious rights of existing non-Jewish communities in Palestine'. The document said nothing of the political or national rights of these communities and didn't name them. Nevertheless, the declaration raised enthusiastic hopes among Zionists and seemed to go some way in fulfilling the aims of the World Zionist Organization. Mandatory Palestine was assigned to Britain in April 1920, with civil administration commencing in July that year. The Mandate was formally in force from 29 September 1923 to 15 May 1948. In the bloodlands of Eastern Europe, still reeling from the aftershocks of the First World War, civil wars, economic hardship, famine and disease, the perennial scourge of antisemitism, here was a glimmer of hope, even in the slimmest of official declarations. For many it was all that was needed.[2]

For a young and idealistic Leo, the dream of building a Jewish homeland was too good an opportunity to miss. At the conclusion of his final school year in June 1920, with the ink not yet dry on his high school diploma, he joined a volunteer socialist Zionist Youth Labour Corps, one of many ventures undertaken by idealistic youth prepared to forsake the land of their birth in pursuit of a dream. Leo travelled to Palestine at the time of the Third Aliyah, the third major wave of modern Zionist immigration from Europe that lasted from 1919 until 1923. Though estimates vary, approximately 35,000 Jews were part of this immigration wave. Triggered by the October Revolution in Russia, antisemitic pogroms in Eastern Europe and the Balfour Declaration, 80 per cent of the pioneers of the Third Aliyah came from Russia and Poland. Most were, like Leo, young 'halutzim' (pioneers) who built roads and towns and drained the marshlands for settlements. Many were members of the socialist 'Hashomer Hatzair' (the Young Guard), a Zionist youth movement founded in 1913 in Galicia, then part of the Austro–Hungarian empire. The movement focused on teaching self-reliance, a love of nature and the outdoor life. It fostered independence and creativity. Most importantly it built a strong Jewish identity that went beyond the stifling confines of Eastern Europe and the restrictions imposed by the rigours of an orthodox Jewish life. All of which spelt freedom for a young man like Leo, eager to explore a brave new world. The Zionist youth of the Third Aliyah were also influenced by a rapidly expanding socialist movement infused with the principles of social justice and equality. These ideals were particularly appealing to young men and women who dreamed of a better, more equitable life in a new land. Leo was no exception.[3]

For two years Leo paved roads in Rosh Pina and worked on kibbutzim, fulfilling the early Zionist ideal of building and developing a Jewish homeland through physical toil and the sweat of one's brow.[4] Rosh Pina in the Upper Galilee was founded in 1882 by 30 pioneering families from Romania, making it one of the oldest Zionist agricultural settlements. In 1883 it came under the patronage of Baron Edmond James de Rothschild.[5] When Leo worked there it had a population of 468, of whom 460 were Jews, four were Muslims and four were Christians.[6] The kibbutz movement consisted of collective farming communities based on socialist principles and an equitable distribution of labour and its proceeds. The first kibbutz, Degania Alef, was established in 1909. In 1922, 700 people were living on kibbutzim, by 1927 the number had risen to 2000. By the outbreak of the Second World War, 5 per cent of the Jewish population of Mandatory Palestine were kibbutzniks.[7] On 19 June 1921 Leo sent a photograph of himself in workman's clothes to his family, writing enthusiastically in schoolboy

Hebrew, 'to my dear parents, brothers and sister, I am sending you a picture in my worker's uniform … I love you, Itzhak, [his Hebrew name] who yearns to see you in the land of Israel'.[8]

Leo wasn't the only one chasing a dream. Of those who embarked on a new life of hope and promise, many went on to forge distinguished careers. The poet and winner of the Israel Prize for literature in 1955, Yitzhak Lamdan immigrated in 1920 as part of the Third Aliyah. He too worked on the land and on kibbutzim before becoming a distinguished writer. The acclaimed poet and journalist Uri Zvi Greenberg arrived in 1923 following a career in the early 1920s as a newspaper editor in Warsaw. Greenberg became a right-wing revisionist and joined the struggle for Israel's independence from British rule. The Hebrew language poet Rachel Bluwstein, known simply by her name Rachel the Poetess, returned to Palestine in 1919. She briefly joined Kibbutz Degania until ill health forced her to leave. She spent the rest of her life in Tel Aviv until her death in 1931.[9]

Between 1921 and 1925, Tel Aviv's population swelled from 3600 to 40,000. Between 1924 and 1926, 40,000 Polish Jews immigrated to Palestine, due to further deteriorating conditions in Poland, rising antisemitism and a steep increase in taxes. But dreams often fall apart in the face of harsh reality. Bloody riots between Arabs and Jews throughout the 1920s destabilised and heightened tensions in the region. By 1925, following a collapse in the economy, 23,000 Jews left Palestine, many disillusioned, unable to make a living. For some, the promise of a land flowing with milk and honey fell painfully short.[10]

Mordechai Fink was able to support his eldest son's dreams and aspirations up to a point. While Leo was open to the promise of a life of hope and ideals, Mordechai did not see a bright future for his idealistic son in a land of struggling pioneers. Tilling the soil while violating the Sabbath, in the Holy Land of all places, was also not in keeping with the religiously observant Masza Fink. Both parents urged him to return to Europe, offering him the opportunity to further his studies in Germany.[11]

The World of Weimar Germany

Following its defeat in the First World War, Germany suffered international isolation. Leo was part of an influx of Eastern Europeans that were welcomed into Germany, helping to fill places at higher educational institutions now left vacant. Germany shared a border with the newly established Second Polish Republic and was easily accessible by an expanding rail network. Leo followed his parents' advice, exchanging his workman's clothes and hand tools for suits and books. But he would forever remain a passionate Zionist, a champion of the Jewish state his entire life. He would return in his later years as a pioneer of a very different kind, chasing another dream.

Leo spent four years in the fast and frenzied world of Weimar Germany, four years that would have exposed him to a very different world of ideas. If Leo's parents entertained any notion that sending him to Germany would provide him with a safe haven, sheltering him from a world of excess and chaos, they picked the wrong place. The Weimar Republic was the name given to the German Government between the Imperial period (1918) and the beginning of Nazi Germany (1933). In the republic's first four years it was plagued by political intrigues, challenged by right- and left-wing factions and was victim to nearly 400 political assassinations.[12]

The Weimar years have been popularly over characterised as a hedonistic period, a jazz age of loose morals that found full expression in the nightlife, gay bars and cabarets of Berlin. Germany was, in the words of writer Klaus Mann 'united not by democracy but by the galvanising rhythm of jazz'.[13] Josephine Baker, the celebrated African American cabaret performer brought her scandalous show 'La Revue Nègre' from Paris to Berlin's 'Theater des Westens' in December 1925. She set the city alight with her 'Dance of the Savages', dressed in a flesh-revealing, flimsy loincloth as well as a skirt composed of bananas, and nothing else. The show received rave reviews; she was dubbed the 'erotic goddess'. It was said that 'the women of Berlin were never the same again'.[14]

The truth is that the Weimar Republic was a period of great achievement, a period of progressive social change and not as weak or ineffective as it is popularly portrayed. Ultimately, it was destroyed and supplanted by a ruthless Nazi dictatorship, but throughout its 15-year rule, it survived many political and economic challenges including coup attempts, counter-revolutions and a communist plot, while absorbing a lost war, economic breakdown and disastrous hyperinflation.

The 'golden age of Weimar' in the mid-1920s, when Leo was there, was a period of some stability, a cultural renaissance, a flourishing period of avant-garde modernism and progressivism, marked by economic recovery, social renewal and cultural innovation. Leo experienced a country and an ethos that embraced change. The pioneering films of Fritz Lang and FW Murnau set a new benchmark in groundbreaking cinema. Murnau's 1922 horror film *Nosferatu*, based on Bram Stoker's *Dracula*, and Lang's 1927 futuristic *Metropolis* are both considered masterpieces of German expressionism. The Bauhaus, founded by modernist architect Walter Gropius in 1919 was an art and design school that revolutionised the way it combined fine art, craft and functionalism. The Weimar Republic was also the most democratic period that Germany ever experienced, with a fiery free press, economic reforms that guaranteed workers an eight-hour day, an unparalleled social welfare system and a public transport network that opened up cities to the surrounding towns and countryside. Women had greater choices than ever before, benefitting from more liberal attitudes towards sex and gender. Intellectually, politically, socially and aesthetically Weimar Germany challenged all preconceived notions of social norms and political conservativism.

But Weimar Germany was also deeply divided. Its great achievements were, ironically, what made it most vulnerable. Liberalisation and progressivism proved to be destabilising for many mainstream Germans craving certainty, order and predictability after the devastation of war. Its emancipatory ethos, its democratic practices, its enlightened art movements, its social mores left it exposed to sustained attacks from conservatives and the radical right. This was the world where the far-right fascist jackboot began its march in 1920, promising a united, greater, all conquering Germany, a Third Reich that would last a thousand years. By the time Leo was in Germany, Hitler was already leading the *Nationalsozialistische Deutsche Arbeiterpartei* (National Socialist German Workers' Party, NSDAP), or the Nazi Party. After 1933 the forces of Nazism crushed all that was free and liberal and progressive.[15]

Weimar Germany of the 1920s was a time of optimism, opportunity, and impending doom. This was the world that Leo entered.

A Student Once More

Armed with a special letter of introduction from Dr Joseph Bloch of Vienna, a friend of his father's, that attested to Leo's good character, his ability to undertake hard work and to the virtues of his idealistic nature, Leo attended Altenburg University for almost two years, from mid-1922 to 1923, where he studied engineering.[16] Altenburg, located 40km south of Leipzig, a town dating back to 976 AD was already well known as a leader in the production of textiles and hardware during the 19th and 20th centuries, especially for its manufacture of sewing machines from companies such as the German-owned Vesta. When Leo was there, Altenburg had a population of 42,000 and was well known as a working-class, industrial city. Leo left Altenburg with a practical understanding of textile machinery, knowledge he would skilfully apply to successful business ventures in coming years. Now he turned his attention to intellectual pursuits.

In 1924 and 1925 Leo attended the prestigious Hochschule für die Wissenschaft des Judentums (Higher Institute for Jewish Studies) in Berlin. A rabbinic seminary established in 1872, its distinguished alumni included Reform Rabbi and theologian Leo Baeck, noted philosopher Emil Fackenheim, founding president of the World Union of Progressive Judaism Claude Montefiore, and academic and educator Solomon Schechter, founder of American Conservative Judaism. Many of the students came from Eastern European countries, notably Poland, as graduates of orthodox yeshivot. By 1921 there were 63 full-time and 45 part-time students enrolled in the Hochschule. In addition to the institute's own curriculum, it was there that Leo is said to have attended lectures by two leading Jewish intellectuals, Einstein and Bialik. The Nobel prize–winning physicist Albert Einstein was also known for his expansive world view which included support for the Zionist cause. The poet, writer and journalist Chaim Nachman Bialik, was a resident of Berlin at the time. A pioneer of modern Hebrew poetry Bialik is best known for his nationalistic poems, notably the stirring 'In the City of Slaughter' which depicted the devastation left in the wake of the 1903 Kishinev pogrom. By the time Leo was 25 years of age, he had been exposed to the world of ideas and influenced by some of the greatest Jewish thinkers of the modern age.

In the mid-1920s Leo found himself in the centre of Germany's political and social whirlwind, a liberal, freethinking yet terrifying world of extremes. It was a Germany still open to and welcoming of Jews, a world where anything seemed possible, a world where you were only limited by your creativity and imagination. But it was also a world teetering on the edge of a precipice, soon to plunge into the heart of fascist darkness.

What becomes of a man once he is launched into the world of ideas? By the time Leo was in his mid-twenties he had seen what could be achieved by personal initiative, was excited by the potential of new social and political movements and understood the power of human endeavour. Bialystok grounded him in the importance of an interconnected Jewish world, the need for personal agency and self-reliance in the struggle for Jewish survival. For six years he lived in two vastly different lands on different continents, Mandatory Palestine and Weimar Germany. Each provided disparate life experiences that were imbued with liberal ideals, that nurtured personal achievement and advancement; a world that was socially progressive and alive with political volatility. Leo was spurred on to broaden his reach, to lead an aspirational life. While the die was cast, Leo's travels and adventures were far from over. There was more to come. More that would define Leo the man.

Chapter 4

NEW BEGINNINGS

It's highly unlikely that the young school girl Mina and the worldly 25-year-old Leo would have crossed paths in 1926. Mina was a 13-year-old in the care of her maternal grandparents in Bialystok, Leo had left the intellectual, progressive, pulsating life of Weimar Germany and was on the move again. But it wasn't back to Bialystok. Fate would bring them together some six years later.

Romania offered a new opportunity for the enterprising, restless Mordechai Fink. At the end of the First World War Romania was an underdeveloped industrial country, 80 per cent of the population still lived in the countryside and the vast majority were involved in some form of agriculture. Democratic reforms within a newly expanded, unified Kingdom of Romania that in 1919 incorporated the neighbouring territories of Transylvania, Bukovina and Bessarabia, allowed for quick economic growth. The country invited foreign investment to finance electric plants, mines, textile mills, foundries, oil wells, roads and rail lines. Industrial production doubled between 1923 and 1938. Mordechai Fink must have thought that his business prospects were better in Romania than Bialystok. Without foreknowledge of Romania, the language or the culture, Mordechai took a leap of faith.[1]

The Fink patriarch went into a business partnership running a spinning and textile factory in Galatz, on the expansive bustling Strada Traian in the heart of an emerging commercial district. Galatz, also known as Galati, was an industrial, trading port city on the Danube river in the historical region of Moldavia, in eastern Romania. Unlike Bialystok, Galatz was not devastated by the First World War, partly because Romania remained neutral for the first two years of the war and while Galatz sustained some shelling in 1918 it didn't destroy the city. It was never occupied by Germany and Romanian soldiers fought alongside the Russian army until the Bolshevik revolution of 1917 saw Russian forces turn on their former Romanian allies. In the Battle for Galatz in January 1918 Romanian troops routed the fragmented Russian army.[2]

By the mid-1920s the population of Galatz was expanding. In 1930 it peaked at 100,000, of which close to 20,000 were Jews, a healthy 20 per cent of the total population, far in excess of the national Romanian average of 4.2 per cent. Jews were active in trade, banking, industry and the crafts. By 1926, the year the Fink family arrived, Galatz was a thriving Jewish centre, home to 22 synagogues, a Talmud Torah, two ritual bathhouses, educational institutions and was the base for the right-wing Zionist Revisionist Organisation of Romania. The community supported a number of Yiddish associations as well as the sports organisations Maccabi and Hagibor. Jewish publications appeared in Yiddish, Romanian and German.[3]

Leo and his three brothers joined their father in this latest, promising enterprise in what was a flourishing Jewish city. It was the first time all four brothers worked together in a business venture, the first of many new beginnings. And although the Romanian business did not fulfil expectations, it provided the Fink brothers with another opportunity. Working together they realised they could be a force to be reckoned with. They also realised that they never wanted to return to life in Bialystok.

Although it is unclear what problems beset the fledgling business, by early 1928 Mordechai Fink decided to abandon his latest venture and head back to Bialystok. Leo had different plans. While reading a Viennese daily newspaper, Leo stumbled upon a leading centrefold article extolling the virtues of a far-off land, 'the land of the future' the paper called it, a land of great opportunity, a land of endless sunshine, Australia. Driven by an overpowering sense of adventure and the hope of a better life, Leo, the spirited pioneer, dispatched a younger brother to the British Embassy in Bucharest to secure entry visas for the brothers.[4] They required £40 for each landing permit and a police certificate attesting to good character and no criminal record. By 9 May 1928 Leo was in possession of both an Australian landing permit and certification from the Police Prefecture of Galati that he was 'of good character in society and not being investigated for any criminal activity'.[5] It was decided that three of the brothers, Leo, Simche (who later anglicised his name to Sid) and Wolf would journey to Australia while the youngest brother Jacob (later Jack) would join them after assisting his parents and sister in their return to Bialystok before undertaking a short practical course in Germany on the management of textile machinery.

Leo, Wolf and Sid embarked on their journey to Australia as soon as transit was available. They booked third-class passage on the steamer SS *Citta di Genova*, an Italian passenger and cargo ship built in 1903.[6] They travelled overland to the port of Constanta in Romania, then by steamship to Alexandria, Egypt completing another 253km overland journey to Port Said, their port of embarkation. Family stories tell of the trials and tribulations endured by the Fink brothers in crossing oceans and desert, of missing travel connections, running out of money, hitchhiking and asking strangers for a meal.[7] But in all this they retained a gritty resolve. They would get to the other end of the earth, come hell or high water.

A Brave New World

Their first glimpse of Australia was the Western Australian port city of Fremantle located at the mouth of the Swan River, a town first settled in 1829 with the first load of convicts arriving on 1 June 1850. It soon became the gateway to the western goldfields and the boom towns of Coolgardie and Kalgoorlie. The Fink brothers were however bound for Melbourne where a Jewish community was already well established. They arrived on 16 June 1928, on a typically fine yet chilly winter's day of 13°C, hardly the freezing snows of a Bialystok winter. Their first registered address was with a Mr B Warth at 442 Drummond Street Carlton, placing them in the heart of a small yet vibrant Yiddish-speaking community.

Carlton, a working-class suburb north of the Yarra River, located close to the markets and factories that offered employment, had been a place of Jewish immigrant settlement since the 1870s. The new influx of Polish Jews strengthened that connection, by 1933 the number of Jews in Carlton nudged 2800, a third of Melbourne's total Jewish population. Carlton's streets were alive with the sound of Yiddish, Polish and Russian. Jewish boarding houses, kosher restaurants, kosher butchers, bakers, grocers, the Kadimah community centre, which housed a communal hall and library, and a number of Eastern European–style synagogues were all concentrated in this one region of the city. Carlton may have cushioned the Yiddish-speaking Fink brothers with a soft, comfortable cultural landing, but the rest of Melbourne was a very foreign place, a far-flung British outpost in the furthest corner of the new world.[8]

The year 1928 was a busy and exciting year for Melburnians. Collingwood won the second of its four consecutive grand finals, beating Richmond by 33 points, Victoria won cricket's Sheffield Shield, and a young 20-year-old batsman Donald Bradman scored his first international test century against England at the Melbourne Cricket Ground. Victoria staged the first Australian Grand Prix at Phillip Island, *Statesman* won the Melbourne Cup, beating the favourite by four lengths and the Melbourne City Council installed the city's first set of traffic lights at the corner of Collins and Swanston streets. There were riots on the wharves when scab labour was used in violation of the Waterside Workers strike and the first pair of 'Speedos' was produced, a distinctive swimming costume featuring a scandalous cut out racerback to allow greater range of motion in the water.

While social customs and an obsession with sport may have been strange and unfamiliar to these Polish Jews, the egalitarianism of early-20th-century Australia was a revelation, a welcome addition to the lives of many Jewish immigrants, affording them a range of opportunities that were not available in their countries of origin. They were free to participate in civil society, could hold public office, enter the professions, engage freely in commerce and the arts, get a full and free education and own property. While Australia, like other Western countries did experience antisemitism, it was not systemic, it did not pose an existential threat, remaining largely popularist and social. There were no pogroms in Melbourne. In relative terms Australia was a safe and secure haven, truly a land of golden opportunities.

In 1921 Melbourne's Jewish population was 6927. Eastern European Jewish immigrants fleeing increasingly difficult times, like the Finks, would increase the Jewish population by another 2000 by the end of the 1920s, a relatively small number but constituting more than the total intake for any previous decade, two-thirds of whom settled in Victoria, predominantly in Melbourne.[9] In 1930, Melbourne's total population reached 1,000,000. Melbourne Jewry constituted less than 1 per cent, a far cry from the high Jewish density of cities like Bialystok.

When Leo and his brothers arrived in Melbourne, the established Melbourne Jewish community that largely resided in the leafy green suburbs south of the Yarra, was the ruling elite. But this community was also in peril of assimilating itself out of existence. Largely a second-generation community, it had a high intermarriage rate that by the 1920s saw one in three Jewish husbands have a non-Jewish wife. Traditional Judaism is matrilineal. Children of non-Jewish mothers are not considered Jewish. The end of the Jewish family was the slippery slide to extinction.[10]

The cultural drive was towards non-distinctiveness. 'Blending in' to a dominant Anglo British way of life was seen not only as a means of diffusing antisemitism but as the ticket to acceptability. The road to successful integration lay in conformity and invisibility. But Leo Fink was no conformist. Certainly not to a British way of life. He would go on to lead a highly visible public Jewish life, he would challenge the Jewish establishment and steer the community in a very different direction. He would marry a life partner who not only shared his vision but would develop as a leader in her own right. Most importantly they shared a love of the Jewish world which they sought to strengthen and replenish. But all of that came later. Leo landed in Melbourne with two of his brothers, little money but a bucketload of drive and ambition, ready to try his hand at just about anything. In an open and free country such as Australia, men like Leo Fink could write their own history.

The Berwick Land Settlement Experiment

The first challenge confronting Leo and his brothers was the desperate need to earn a living. Their father had been able to pay their landing permits and their passage but now they were left to their own devices. While the financial crisis of the Great Depression was yet to engulf the world, by 1928 there were signs of a weakening economy. In 1920s Victoria, factories came to surpass rural industries as the main generator of wealth but it was increasingly difficult for immigrants to find work in the factories and markets.[11] Of the 2000 Jewish immigrants who landed in Melbourne, the rush came between 1926 and 1928, placing a significant burden on philanthropic organisations. The Victorian Jewish Welcome Society, formed in 1922 by an earlier wave of Eastern Europeans keen to help new arrivals, was buckling under the pressure.

The need to secure suitable employment, accommodation and provide basic English lessons forced another solution to be found. 'Jews as Farmers: Solving Australian Jewish Immigration Problem' the *Hebrew Standard of Australasia* proudly claimed on 24 August 1928. Putting the new arrivals on the land seemed like a good idea. It would solve the housing and employment problem in one fell swoop and also relieve a number of other pressing issues. If left homeless and unemployed in the city, a highly visible foreign element might resort to being 'peddlers or hawkers', unsightly occupations that would only reinforce ugly stereotypes. On the other hand, if Jews were conspicuously engaged in agriculture, working productively on the land, it would diminish any chance of escalating antisemitism. It was also thought that it would enable the smooth integration of Jewish immigrants into an Australian way of life, as Australian identity was closely tied to a muscular, robust image of men working the land.[12] A very nervous Jewish establishment thought it had found the perfect solution to its immigrant dilemma. Out of sight and out of mind.[13]

The successful Shepparton land experiment which commenced in 1913 saw Jewish immigrants develop large and productive orchards.[14] A similar model was adopted in 1927 for a large tract of land in nearby Berwick, only 45km from the city. This would be developed as market gardens or poultry farms, allowing for a quick return for effort rather than having to wait for years while orchards reached maturity as they did at Shepparton. The land at Berwick was fertile for vegetable growing and roads and rail made the transportation of produce relatively straightforward. An ambitious fundraising effort was launched to underwrite the scheme. Melbourne's Jewish establishment embraced the notion and initially supported the fundraising.[15]

Leo, Sid and Wolf joined some 25 Jewish families comprising 60 individuals who tilled blocks averaging 19 acres each. But the Fink brothers were urban Jews, more at home amongst the textile mills and smokestacks of Eastern Europe than behind a plough. In spite of all efforts, and a successful tomato crop, the first Fink enterprise failed. This was not entirely their fault.[16] The Berwick experiment was a bold plan that hit a number of obstacles. The main culprit was the Wall Street Crash of 1929. It frightened off investors and shrank the market for primary produce. By 1930 immigration to Australia was increasingly difficult as effects of the Depression gripped the country and the government was forced to put the brakes on. The flood of Jewish refugees became a trickle negating the need to find accommodation and employment. But perhaps the main obstacle was the lack of a Jewish communal centre as a focal point that could encourage and sustain a vibrant community, a Jewish heart that would pump life into these often lonely, homesick immigrants. Isolation was the enemy.

A few short months after the youngest Fink brother Jack joined them, arriving on 15 February 1929, the Finks abandoned all expectations for a future on the land. Armed with a second-hand machine called a 'ragger', which shredded and recycled fabric, sent with Jack and bought by their father Mordechai, the four brothers returned to Melbourne to explore business opportunities. Other more established 'newcomers' stepped up and gave assistance. Successful wine merchant, Polish-born Sammy Wynn, who arrived in 1913, acted as guarantor for a bank loan. Russian-born Yasha Taft, an electrical contractor who arrived in 1922, helped set up the textile machine, refusing any payment, suggesting they 'pay him when they can'. Out of a small rented room in a Carlton boarding house, they worked the one machine continually through day and night shifts. From small beginnings do great things grow. The Fink brothers' enterprise never looked back.[17]

Business Expansion as the Depression Bites

By 1931 business was good for Leo and his brothers. They were manufacturing felt and knitted goods out of a rented factory on Queens Parade in Clifton Hill. Business was so good in fact that they planned to further expand their Melbourne enterprise. Fink Bros Pty Ltd, now in partnership with fellow Bialystoker Michael Pitt, authorised a credit note on 2 March 1931 for the sum of £1500 to send Leo to Europe to buy machinery.[18] At this time, business expansion of such a magnitude was a considerable achievement. The Great Depression had driven unemployment in Australia to a record 32 per cent. Only a damaged, war-ravaged Germany suffered higher unemployment.

The catastrophic downturn in the world economy was transferred to Australia by falling export prices and sales and the decline in overseas loans exacerbated unemployment. The incidence of unemployment was however uneven, hitting some sectors of the economy harder than others. Melbourne suffered more than the rest of Victoria, and men more than women. The unskilled suffered more than the skilled and Catholics more than other religions. More than half of all building workers lost their jobs compared with less than one in eight professionals. Civil servants largely escaped the Depression unscathed. Few farmers were driven off the land or were unemployed. They worked harder for smaller profit but survived the worst. Poorer suburbs were hardest hit, as were people aged 20 to 29 or over 40. By 1933 almost a third of all unemployed men had been without work for three years. Thousands left Melbourne by train, foot or bicycle living rough or in hastily erected tent cities, in the hope of finding itinerant work in the countryside. Private charities struggled to meet the huge demand. Governments instigated relief works. Those who had no work were given a small weekly sum called 'sustenance', barely enough to buy food. To receive the 'susso' was however viewed with distain and disgust by many, a blow to self-esteem for men who never had to survive on handouts, men who had survived the trenches and Gallipoli, men who saw themselves as family providers. Later they were put to work creating suburban parks, the Yarra Boulevard, the Shrine of Remembrance and other public works. Fortunately, no bank in Victoria crashed, there was no rush on withdrawals fuelled by panic and fear. A resurgent manufacturing sector led the recovery but it wasn't until the outbreak of the Second World War that unemployment numbers were dramatically slashed.[19] And yet amidst the turmoil, hardship and uncertainty of these times, Leo Fink and his brothers, now budding entrepreneurs, manufacturers and businessmen, thrived.

Leo and Mina – A 'Match made' Marriage

Leo planned his business trip to include a substantial stay in Bialystok where he would seek to purchase textile machinery and visit his parents and sister, who now resided at 25 Czestochowa Street. It would be the last time he ever set foot in Bialystok but its consequences would change his life forever.

In June 1932, 19-year-old Miriam (Mina) Waks was preparing to graduate from the prestigious Druskin Gymnasium. She aspired to further her education at university in Warsaw, but fate intervened. Leo's mother Masza, the religious matriarch of the family was concerned that her 31-year-old eldest son was still a bachelor. 'I haven't had time to find a wife', Leo explained to his disapproving mother. She offered to act as matchmaker, an offer Leo accepted. Masza Fink found three suitable candidates, all of whom she felt would make good companions. One came from a family of good standing, another was educated. But the third one in particular stood out. The young, pretty, educated Mina, who had been orphaned at a young age, was the preferred candidate. To marry an orphan was a 'mitzvah' a good deed, his mother advised. Leo agreed. On her grandmother Brajna Kaplan's advice, Mina also settled on the match, in full knowledge that it would take her far from the home she knew and loved, dashing all hopes for a university education. While Leo cut an unimposing figure – he was short in stature and wore heavy horn-rimmed glasses – he nevertheless made a favourable impression. He was a good man from a good family, educated, with excellent prospects, and a fellow Bialystoker. Mina trusted her intuition, as Leo trusted his. On 20 September 1932, Leo and Mina became husband and wife. It was the beginning of a fulfilling partnership that enriched both their lives and the lives of so many others.[20]

A New Life, a New Home

The newly married couple arrived in Melbourne on 29 November 1932 aboard the Royal Mail Steamer *Orama*, which operated passenger, cargo and mail services between England and Australian ports from 1924 until it was sunk in 1940 amidst the turmoil of war. Their port of embarkation was Naples. They travelled third class. It was the first time Mina had set foot outside of her native Poland. It awakened in her a sense of adventure, one she would share with her husband. She relished the opportunity to cross the seas and would throughout her lifetime become an intrepid traveller, crisscrossing the globe visiting extended family and an ever-widening circle of friends.

Their first place of residence was listed on the ship's manifest as 33 Gipps Street, East Melbourne, what was then a small, single-storey workman's cottage, but now part of prime inner-city real estate. Before long they were able to move into more salubrious accommodation. From 1933 to 1939, the Finks lived at 99 Walpole Street in the Melbourne suburb of Kew, in a house rented from the Lord Mayor. Kew derived its name from the site of Kew gardens in England and was described in 1865 'as the most picturesque portion of the suburbs of Melbourne'. Due to council policy that limited industry, Kew only had 29 factories in 1927. Hawthorn had 140. Kew was decidedly middle class, green and leafy. But not all Kew residents lived well during those times. In 1931, £8000 in sustenance orders were made to Kew residents suffering from the impact of the Depression.[21]

Although only a short distance to the more familiar working-class inner-city suburbs of Collingwood and Abbotsford, a Kew address signalled a speedy upward mobility for the now affluent Leo and his young wife Mina. Both were aspirational, but never flashy or flamboyant. Respectability was prized and Mina would, throughout her life, value the trappings of a good life that enabled her to serve the needs of others for whom life was not so good.

During Leo and Mina's time in Walpole Street, the house became a lively, welcoming home to a host of extended family members. Leo's youngest brother Jack would live with them until he married Sadie Krause in 1935. Mina and Sadie would become close, lifelong friends and co-workers in charitable causes close to both their hearts. Mina's two brothers Jack and Leo Waks took up residence when they arrived from Poland in 1937, after being sponsored by their brother-in-law who acted as guarantor. Family photos reveal their two makeshift beds set up on the balcony of the Fink home. It was the home that welcomed Leo and Mina's two children. Mina gave birth to their daughter Freda on 18 September 1933 and their son Nathan on 21 January 1935. While still in her early twenties, Mina had undergone dramatic upheavals in her life. She had been orphaned, become a wife, an immigrant and a mother of two. In all this, her strength of character prevailed.

The 1930s was a period of rapid growth and personal development. Mina was learning to navigate her new environment. She was now a loving member of the Fink clan. She embraced them as they did her. She learnt to speak, read and write English, though for the remainder of her life she regretted never being as proficient in her adopted language as she would have liked. Polish would remain her first 'official' language, Yiddish the language of home, family and community. She became an exemplary wife and hostess, quickly gaining a reputation for her newly acquired culinary skills, her impeccably well-groomed appearance, her fashion sense and her exceptional organisational ability. She developed a broad circle of friends, a network of women who would volunteer to work with her throughout her life. As in all things she undertook, near enough was never good enough. Mina set exacting standards for herself and others. It was how her grandparents raised her, it was how she did things. All of this stood her in good stead for the years ahead in which circumstance and necessity would propel her into a life of unrelenting service.

Leo was also beginning to flex his communal muscle. In 1936 he began his long association with the Kadimah, the most important communal organisation representing the rapidly growing Yiddish-speaking community. Established on 26 December 1911, the Kadimah was the centre of Jewish immigrant life in Carlton. Leo was co-opted as a committee member. For Mina, it made perfect sense. At that time 'there was nothing [other than the Kadimah] in the Jewish community that I particularly wanted to be a part of'.[22]

By 1938 Leo was elected treasurer, a position he executed with distinction and one that raised his community profile. It was no surprise that this was the first place in which Leo's considerable leadership skills were put to the test. It was a year in which the Kadimah embarked on a program of growth and development.

The Fink business continued to grow. In 1935 Leo was joint managing director of United Woollen Mills Pty Ltd now located at 211 Sturt Street, South Melbourne. The company manufactured blankets, woollen and worsted materials. Prosperity was the great enabler. It allowed Leo and Mina to sponsor family members desperate to abandon an increasingly hostile Poland and come to Australia. Chain migration was a common pattern of immigration, enabling large families to immigrate together or in clusters. Pre-war Jewish families, like the Finks, utilised the same process. The Australian Government did not provide financial assistance to Jewish immigrants. And just as they had learnt in the 'old country', it came down to Jews helping other Jews. Survival depended on it. Often one member of the family, or someone from the same town or region would travel first, establishing the first link in the chain. Others would be brought out as soon as the first member was established and financially secure. So it was with the Finks. Mina had brought her brothers to Melbourne in 1937 and her uncle Jacob Waks, who was issued a landing permit in 1939, and fortuitously managed to reach Melbourne in 1940, by which time Europe was burning.

The Fink brothers went to extraordinary lengths to bring their parents and disabled sister to Australia after their visa applications were initially refused. But Leo was never one to take no for an answer. Without hesitation, he travelled to Canberra to put the family's case, guaranteeing that their elderly parents and disabled sister would not be a burden on the State. The Finks could and would provide financial and social support. Permits were granted. They arrived in mid-December 1935, also on the *Orama*, the same ship that brought Leo and Mina on their first voyage as husband and wife. Mordechai, Masza and Zyna took up residence at 955 Rathdowne Street, North Carlton. And as she had undertaken with the Fink brothers, Mina embraced them as her own. Between 1929 and 1939 some 20 members of the Fink family arrived in Melbourne as a direct result of family sponsorship. In reality it simply came down to one thing; they cared. Deeply.[23]

Amidst a growing family and a busy home life, Mina proved herself to be accomplished, adaptable and resilient. And yet, in spite of all that was good, the welcoming Finks, a devoted husband, a young family, she was overwhelmed by a nagging emptiness. Like many immigrants before and after her, Mina became homesick. Very homesick. She desperately needed to once more see and feel the warmth of the family who had raised her. She felt the urge to once more walk the streets of Bialystok, to breathe its air, to be amongst the old, the familiar and not the strange newness of a world tipped upside down. Leo understood. She needed to make her peace with it all, as he had years earlier. They booked their passage, placed their two young children into the loving care of Jack and Sadie Fink. As the world was rapidly hurtling towards its descent into hell, they set out. In March 1938 Hitler swallowed up Austria in the Anschluss. And Mina returned to Bialystok.

Chapter 5

ON THE BRINK

Three weeks was all the time Mina had in Bialystok. Three weeks to reconcile a life once lived and a life to be lived. Mina travelled alone into Bialystok in March 1938, leaving Leo in Europe, where he awaited her return.[1] While Leo understood Mina's need to return to Bialystok, he no longer had to feel its physical presence. Leo carried what he needed of Bialystok deep in his soul. He also intuitively knew this was a trip that Mina needed to do alone.

Mina travelled by train across an increasingly belligerent Germany, her only companion being Hitler's menacing voice booming out from the radio. It was a harrowing experience she never forgot. 'It sent shivers down my spine', she recalled many times over the years. Back in Australia the newspapers took a dim view of what was happening in Germany, its annexation of Austria and its impact on the Jews. 'Ruthless attacks on Jews, Nazis continue purge in Austria', *The Argus* reported on 21 March 1938. The front page of the same paper had a photograph of a crowd of cheering Austrians, enthusiastically giving the Nazi salute outside the Chancellery in Vienna, 'while it sings the German national anthem'.

When Mina arrived in Bialystok, she was shocked by the deterioration in living conditions in Poland. 'It was terrible there', she recalled. A pervasive sense of fear and uncertainty hung heavily in the air. These were dangerous times.

Polish Antisemitism Surges

By 1938 the lives of Polish Jews had taken a dramatic turn for the worse. With the death of popular Polish leader, the military hero and strongman Marshal Jozef Pilsudski in 1935, what had been a brief period of some stability for the Jews came to an abrupt end. Anti-Jewish sentiment reached its zenith in the years leading up to the Second World War. The rapid rise of Polish nationalism dragged the very presence of Jews back into the centre of the political arena. With the rising influence of the radical right-wing Endecja party throughout Poland, a more lethal form of government-sanctioned antisemitism swiftly gathered momentum. Between 1935 and 1937, 79 Jews were killed and 500 injured in anti-Jewish incidents.[2]

Discriminatory measures specifically designed to discourage participation in educational institutions were put into law and brutally enforced. 'Ghetto benches', the official segregation in the seating of Jewish and non-Jewish university students was introduced in 1935 at the Lwow Polytechnic, followed by its legalisation throughout the Polish Republic in 1937. This was often accompanied by violence, abuse and harassment if Jewish students refused to sit in their designated seats. Even when they did, they were not immune from indiscriminate attacks. The practice continued until the outbreak of war. Universities often exercised official and unofficial quotas which more than halved the total number of Jewish students from 20.4 per cent in 1918 to 7.5 per cent in 1937.[3]

Jews were excluded from positions in the government-controlled civil service, they were unable to participate in Polish trade unions and could not claim state-funded welfare. In 1936 the Ministry of Commerce ordered that signs on stores and establishments display the name of the owners as they appeared on birth certificates, effectively support-ing an anti-Jewish boycott by making it easier for customers to avoid Jewish enterprises. Violence frequently targeted Jewish stores, many were routinely looted. The most popular Polish slogan was 'beat up a Jew'. It could be heard on the streets, marketplaces and city centres. Even when left unspoken, its pervasive, odorous presence could be felt. Persistent economic boycotts coupled with the lingering effects of the Great Depression saw a substantial portion of Polish Jews living in grinding poverty until the war irrevocably sealed their fate.[4]

Catholic organisations and the Catholic press were amongst the most effective disseminators of antisemitic venom. Catholic priests were among the most prolific authors of antisemitic propaganda. One of the first lessons Polish children learnt from their priests was that the Jews had killed Christ. The old blood libel, that Jews practised ritual murder of defenceless Christians, especially children, reared its ugly head again, and was unquestioningly accepted by the Polish masses. In 1936 the Primate of Poland openly supported anti-Jewish policies and publicly stated that the only salvation for the Jews was their conversion.[5]

On 7 February 1937 the *New York Times* reporter Otto D Tolischus, one of the paper's most experienced international correspondents reported on the alarming deterioration in living conditions in what had been Leo and Mina's hometown; 'in Bialystok alone there had occurred during the last year 348 assaults on Jews including 21 mass riots or pogroms, 99 cases of Jew baiting, 161 cases of window smashing ... 3 Jews were killed and 7 severely injured'. Towards the end of his article, he made the ominous prophesy; 'Antisemitism, raised by Adolf Hitler in Germany to the status of a political religion, is rapidly spreading throughout eastern Europe and is thereby turning the recurrent Jewish tragedy in that biggest Jewish centre in the world [Poland] into a final disaster of truly historic magnitude'. Tolischus would go on to win a Pulitzer prize in 1940 for his work in reporting from Berlin.

In 1938 the Polish parliament raised the issue of banning the kosher ritual slaughter of animals and the Diet legislated to outlaw it altogether by 1942.[6] Only the war halted its implementation. By the time Mina returned to Bialystok, the Jewish population was being systematically strangled, having the life squeezed out of it by forces determined to remove the Jewish presence once and for all.

This was the 'new' Poland Mina now confronted. This was her home-coming. Mina's reunion with family and friends was nevertheless heartfelt but also bittersweet. Photos of the reunion show smiling faces and happy gatherings. On the back of one photo Mina wrote 'sweet memories of 1938'. While family and friends embraced their beloved Mina, they also pleaded with her to get as many of the children out of the country as possible. Mina promised to do all she could but it was a pledge she was unable to fulfil. By the time Mina and Leo returned from their trip abroad time had run out.

No Escape

Time wasn't Mina's only enemy. By 1939 it was exceedingly difficult for Polish Jews to find refuge in Australia. Only a small number of Jews who arrived in Australia in 1938 and 1939 were Polish or from other Eastern European countries. In response to the November 1938 German pogrom that became known as Kristallnacht, the night of broken glass, the Australian Government made a commitment to admit 15,000 Jews over three years. But the government prioritised that the 5000 per annum be refugees, defined narrowly as nationals or former nationals of Germany, Austria or Czechoslovakia. Jewish refugees were not to exceed 4000 and the other 1000 were to be 'non-Aryan

Christian' refugees, defined as those Jews who had converted to Christianity. Under mounting pressure to do more, on 27 April 1939 the government granted another 1000 places for 'non-refugee' Eastern European Jews, on condition they were sponsored by a relative. In effect Eastern European Jews had to compete for less than 20 per cent of the available places. All this had to take place over a short four-month period in 1939, from late April to September when war broke out.[7] Mina's inability to have acted sooner and faster haunted her for the rest of her life. 'I could have saved more lives', she lamented.[8] In truth, there was little she could have done.

It was the last time Mina saw her remaining family, friends or Bialystok. She never returned. There would be nothing to return to. And like Leo, Bialystok would forever remain a part of her, locked deep in the recesses of her heart, in her soul. It was where Mina, the 8-year-old orphan, had laid her parents to rest. Now her past had found its own resting place.

Back Home

Mina and Leo returned to Australia via New York where they met up with Leo's American cousin Mack Glickfeld, crossing the North Atlantic on board the RMS *Queen Mary*, a British ocean liner that sailed from 1936 to 1967 for the Cunard line. It was the fastest luxury liner of its kind in 1938, boasting cutting-edge facilities and an art deco interior design. Photographs of Leo and Mina attest to a shipboard life that was replete with black tie dinners, lively company and elegant surrounds.

On their return, Leo and Mina moved from a rented house into a bought property at 5 Berkeley Court, Kew, a prime location off Studley Park Road. In the lead-up to the outbreak of war, a comfortable, safe life for the Fink family in Melbourne was still a world away from the dark clouds that hung over Europe. Life was good.

Jewish Life in Melbourne

By 1938 everyday life for the 9000 Jews of Melbourne was culturally rich, politically diverse and complex. The warp and weft of Eastern European Jewish life, of which Leo and Mina were so closely tied, had woven itself into the fabric of Jewish Melbourne. The 3000 Yiddish speakers who immigrated to Melbourne in the early part of the 20th century were re-establishing their own world, complete with its distinct culture, combustible politics and self-help organisations, a world that Leo and Mina knew well and fully supported. These 'newcomers' mostly lived in the working-class suburbs north of the Yarra River. Melbourne's well established Anglo Jewish community preferred to live their lives as discreetly as possible, under the cover of invisibility, blending in rather than standing out. For them, home lay in the leafy residential suburbs south of the Yarra. For conservative establishment Jews, many of whom could trace their Australian roots back several generations with some boasting First Fleet convict ancestry, flying under the radar was seen to be the antidote to antisemitism. On the other hand, the Yiddish speakers of Eastern Europe lived highly visible lives, their cultural distinctiveness seen as a badge of honour. At the core of this dichotomy was the issue of identity and what it meant to be a Jew in a rapidly changing Jewish community in Melbourne, Australia. For Jews like Leo and Mina, cultural visibility was an important part of Jewish continuity. How could you survive if you could not be seen? Or heard? Or counted?

In the heartland of Yiddish Carlton sat the Kadimah, first established in 1911 and now the Jewish 'newcomers' rapidly expanding cultural centre. By the late 1930s the Kadimah was also a social hub, boasting an expansive library, hosting literary and musical evenings, an extensive public lecture program, an active and engaged youth group and very successful fundraising initiatives. A vibrant Yiddish theatre was now being celebrated and applauded, playing to sellout crowds in the 400-seat Kadimah hall, a Yiddish newspaper was successfully launched in 1935 after several false starts and a Yiddish school, named after the Yiddish writer IL Peretz, opened in 1935 with classes on Wednesday afternoons and Sunday mornings. The essential components of a life once lived in Poland was now being replicated in this furthest corner of the world.

The Kadimah quickly established itself as a political force and rightful representative of this Jewish immigrant community. In 1938, with Leo as treasurer, the Kadimah pushed for greater representation on and democratisation of the self-appointed, autocratic Victorian Jewish Advisory Board (VJAB). The VJAB was an organisation that claimed to represent all Victorian Jewry, but its exclusive power base lacked transparency, was led by three synagogues: East Melbourne, Toorak and St Kilda and remained largely removed from the ordinary lives of the new immigrants. It lacked relevancy. The issue of representation would only be resolved piecemeal, without full resolution until 1942.[9] Leo helped lead the charge for democratic reform.

The heated politics of Bund versus Zionism was vigorously played out in Melbourne as it had been in Eastern Europe. In Australia the Zionist movement gained widespread popularity in the interwar period, consolidated in the formation of state bodies and in 1927, a national federation. It attracted wide support, including Jewish 'celebrities' such as Sir John Monash and Major Isidor Isaacson, a Boer War and First World War veteran. Zionism would be championed by Eastern

European Jews such as Samuel Wynn and Leo and Mina Fink. The Bund was officially launched in Melbourne in 1928 by a small influential group of Jewish immigrants. As it had done in Eastern Europe, Melbourne's Bund was mandated by its socialist ideals and its support of the Yiddish language and its literature. Yiddish remained a cultural identity marker. The Bund's small numbers would never eclipse those of the Zionist movement's juggernaut but it remained an influential organisation that would leave its mark on Jewish Welfare initiatives and which forged strong, important links with the Australian Labor Party.[10]

Concerns Mount for Polish Jews

While the troubles confronting Jews in an increasingly hostile world were being fomented in Europe, in Melbourne a rich and diverse Jewish life remained largely unencumbered by the realities of a perilous world hurtling towards self-destruction. But concern was mounting. For Jews with strong ties to the Eastern European Jewish world, the warning bells rang loud and clear. The Polish Jewish Relief Fund (PJRF), of which Leo Fink was a leading committee member, was founded in Melbourne in 1935 by a group of Polish Jewish immigrants to raise funds for destitute Polish Jews. In response to worsening conditions in Poland, the PJRF decided on a direct intervention. Its most robust and daring plan was the rescue of 20 Polish Jewish male orphans aged 15 and 16. The task involved negotiation with the Australian Government and the overseas Jewish relief organisation, the ORT-OZE, responsible for selecting the boys and their welfare. Negotiations were protracted, taking two years to reach fruition. The PJRF arranged their landing permits and welfare guarantees. The boys arrived in Melbourne on 28 May 1939, just three months before the outbreak of war. Of the 20 boys, 16 would go on to serve in the Australian armed forces during the Second World War. It proved once again that the road to Jewish survival depended on self-help and self-reliance. It also gave Leo the first taste of social action with tangible human outcomes.[11]

Life in the 'Other' Melbourne

For other Melburnians, the vast majority of whom had never left these shores, the European continent remained a distant site of immeasurable grief and loss, a World War I graveyard where a generation of young Australian men lay entombed.

It was only 20 years since the end of the Great War, a war in which 330,000 Australians served on distant shores with a staggering 60,000 casualties, at a time when Australia's population was just 5 million. Of these 112,000 were Victorians, 16,000 of whom were killed. That war was part of living memory for the vast majority of Australians. Its human cost was still present in the lives and living rooms of many Australians, all of whom lost loved ones or knew of others sacrificed to serve King and country. Photographs of young men lost to war, gas masks that hung on the walls of family homes, picture postcards from France that often adorned the mantlepieces of suburbia were bleak reminders that Australia was not immune from the madness of a distant world. As the historian Kate Darian-Smith pointed out, 'The First World War lived on in songs, Anzac Day parades, the wards of repatriation hospitals, and public begging by maimed survivors wearing signs with messages like "Gassed" or "Gallipoli"'.[12]

Little wonder there was no appetite for what was shaping up as another overseas conflict. Little wonder that Melburnians did their best to shut out the troubles of the world. Life went on, with energy and fervour.

By 1938 Melbourne was Australia's second largest city, and the nation's financial centre with a population now tipping over 1,000,000. It was a sprawling metropolis, with the metropolitan area covering 105 square kilometres, home to imposing public buildings that stood as reminders of the prosperity brought by the gold rush. Electric trams were replacing the cable cars of the last century, Flinders Street Station had thousands of commuters pass under its row of clocks daily. Bourke Street was the retail hub. Cinemas and theatres catered to enthusiastic crowds while pubs remained popular meeting places. Suburbs fanned out in all directions, falling into socio-economic divisions. Working classes lived in the inner municipalities with high population densities. Housing conditions were poor. Light to medium industry was located in the northern areas, heavy industry to the west. East and south of the Yarra River housed the majority of Melburnians, with suburbs such as Camberwell and Caulfield having undergone rapid development in the 1920s.[13]

The cultural scene was buzzing with many 'firsts'. In 1938 the controversial artist, writer and cartoonist Norman Lindsay whose many works were deemed blasphemous, published *Age of Consent* in Britain. It portrayed a scandalous relationship between a middle-aged painter and an adolescent girl. It was banned in Australia until 1962. In the same year, Ken Hall's comedy film *Dad and Dave Come to Town* was released on 30 September, the third in the Dad and Dave series. Variety magazine said 'it broke all records everywhere' and premiered in the United Kingdom as *The Rudd Family Goes to Town*. It was the first Australian film to screen in the West End and received rave reviews. It was the year in which Nora Heysen became the first woman to win the prestigious Archibald Prize for portraiture.

Amidst the distant rumblings of a European continent bracing itself for what would be the deadliest global conflict of the modern era, Victoria's start to 1939 was marred by catastrophic bushfires. Fuelled by years of drought, searing temperatures over 40°C and strong winds, what became known as Black Friday claimed the lives of 71 Victorians. Smoke covered the entire state and ash fell as far away as New Zealand. Approximately 1300 buildings were lost – more than 700 homes, 69 sawmills, many businesses, farms and other buildings.[14]

Recovery was slow but Aussies showed their usual resilience. While still reeling from the devastation of the fires, without full recovery from the Great Depression, amidst the lingering shadow of the Great War, Australia soon found itself on the frontline of world events once again.

At 9:15pm on 3 September 1939 in a radio broadcast to the nation, the prime minister Robert Menzies told the Australian people that 'it is my melancholy duty to inform you officially that, in consequence of the persistence of Germany in her invasion of Poland, Great Britain has declared war upon her, and that, as a result, Australia is also at war'.[15]

The solemn announcement asked the nation to steel itself for a new conflict. While Australians would quickly respond to the call to arms, they were, at this stage, urged to get on 'with business as usual'. As the country became increasingly placed on a war footing, news leaking out from Europe about the plight of the Jews was devastating. As early as October and November 1939, the Jewish press were employing terms such as 'annihilation', 'extermination' and 'extinction'.

For Leo and Mina 'business as usual' was not an option.

Chapter 6

'A MATTER
OF LIFE AND DEATH'

In 1942 everything changed. It was the year that Hitler unleashed the 'Final Solution', the ultimate plan to systematically murder all of Europe's Jews. What began with mass shootings in 1941 was quickly superseded by a more lethal and efficient means of extermination. Six Nazi death camps were established in Poland. By March 1943, 4 million Jews, already weakened by years of starvation and disease, had been murdered. That number would rise to 6 million by war's end.[1]

News reports painted a grim picture of the relentless, indiscriminate slaughter taking place in the towns and cities that Jews like Leo and Mina had once called home. The Kadimah, the spiritual home for immigrant Jews, recognised the gravity of the situation:

> We are carrying on our work in an atmosphere in which the greatest tragedy in human history is being enacted. The culture and material values of Europe are being engulfed by the savage onslaught of the Nazi Fascist hordes and over two thirds of the entire Jewish population of the world is faced with extermination by murder.[2]

In 1942, Leo and Mina Fink began their ascent into the leadership roles that would come to define them. 'Something had to be done ... We could not accept the situation with resignation', Leo declared. 'It was a matter of life and death', Mina explained.[3]

While 1942 was a decisive turning point, by then the war against the Jews had already been underway for three gruelling, bloody years. Jews in occupied territories were targeted from day one. The emotional toll on Melbourne's immigrant Jews was great as the fate of family and friends trapped in a Europe that was tearing itself apart, was difficult to ascertain. Letters went unanswered. Telegrams undelivered. Contact was cut. It was quickly understood that this was a deadly war waged against all Jews, regardless of where they lived. Hitler's rhetoric made it clear that all Jews were potential targets for extermination, the 'ultimate goal' Hitler proclaimed in an early pre-war speech, 'must definitely be the removal of the Jews altogether'. Sir Samuel Cohen a leader of New South Wales Jewry in the 1930s and a member of the Jewish 'establishment' acknowledged that 'many of us have roots in Australia from the very early days. I have looked upon myself as an Australian of the Jewish faith. Unfortunately, it is different in Europe and Hitler aims to show us as a race apart'.[4] For Australian Jewry this was a deeply personal war. For those with close ties to Europe, the impact was devastating. 'We all lost someone', Mina recalled.[5]

Australia Goes to War

In the early days of the conflict Melbourne bore little resemblance to a city at war. Evidence points to an early period of optimism. Holiday sites recorded a boom period throughout December 1939 and January 1940. The New Year of 1940 was ushered in with record crowds celebrating in the streets of the capital cities, unexpected high sales were recorded by retailers and Don Bradman scored his 90th century at the Melbourne Cricket Ground. Australia may have been at war but its citizens were not.[6]

Recruitment offices opened in October 1939 and in January 1940 Victoria's AIF battalions proudly marched through the city streets to the largest crowds ever assembled. Soldiers were cheered by enthusiastic crowds and wellwishers mingled with these newest armed forces as they embarked for the distant shores of the Middle East. For those on the home front, the war, which already had such a profound impact on Melbourne Jewry, was still physically and psychologically far removed. But not for long.[7]

Any sense of security felt by Australians in those early heady years, that this was largely an overseas conflict, quickly evaporated. In 1942, the Pacific war landed on Australian shores. The fall of Singapore on 15 February 1942 delivered the largest British surrender in history. The entire 8th Division of the AIF was captured. Morale plummeted. But worse was still to come. On 19 February Darwin was bombed, 243 people were killed. For the first time Australia came under direct enemy attack.[8] This island nation of 7 million inhabitants, thought to be safely perched at the edge of the world, was suddenly exposed and vulnerable. Now the war was on our doorstep. An unstoppable Japanese army appeared invincible as it pushed on through South-East Asia. Would Australia be next? On 25 February 1942 Leo finalised his Will, ensuring his wife and children would be provided for, should the worst come to pass.[9]

Melbourne quickly transitioned to being a city at war. Air raid trenches appeared, as did sandbags in the streets, ration coupons were distributed, war loans were advertised, the military requisitioned buildings and there was the 'brown out', the symbol of war time domestic mobilisation when street lights were turned off or hooded and windows covered to protect the city from anticipated Japanese night-time aerial attacks. But it was the appearance of large numbers of men and women in uniform, the tearful farewells on the train platforms in full knowledge that it could be their last embrace, that dominated a city now in the grip of a brutal global conflict.[10]

Australian Jews Answer the Call

Right from the start Australian Jewry gave unequivocal support to the war effort. A victory over Hitler would certainly put an end to the carnage against the Jews while protecting Australia's sovereignty and democratic freedoms. Shortly before the outbreak of hostilities in August 1939, Rabbi Falk, acting chief minister of Sydney's Great Synagogue told his radio listeners that 'should the hour strike when the Empire calls its sons to defend its flag, Israel will respond with a mighty "Here I am"'.[11] In an article published in the *Australian Jewish Herald* just four days after war was declared with Germany, the Victorian Jewish Advisory Board pledged Australian Jewry's commitment to the fight against fascism; 'We stand united … the community places all its resources behind those who fight for civilisation and human rights'.[12] Archie Michaelis, president of the Victorian Jewish Advisory Board and himself a war veteran who lost his brother and three first cousins in the Great War, sent a letter to the director of recruiting in which he gave the community's 'energetic support of the campaign for recruits'.[13] The Kadimah too urged its members to 'be ready for duty and service to our country and to our people in whatever capacity we are called upon to serve'.[14] And just as they had done during that 'war to end all wars', Australian Jews answered the call to enlist. Some 5260 Jewish servicemen and women, representing all walks of life and an enlistment rate of 17.5 per cent, significantly higher than the national rate of 10 per cent, stood ready to defend the Australian way of life, a life that had given them all the rights of full citizenship, unheard of in the far-off lands of their ancestors. Australian Jewish servicemen and women received 120 wartime awards for bravery and conspicuous service.[15]

Leo and Mina did not stand idly by. Loyalty, duty and a commitment to the country that had served them so well was unconditional. They were determined to do their bit.

When the call for mobilisation went out following the outbreak of war in September 1939, Leo was already enlisted in the Army Reserve 24/39 Battalion. As the early rumblings of an imminent war grew ever louder and a belligerent, militaristic Germany and Japan were rapidly expanding their territories, Leo took the initiative and offered his services with the volunteer reserve militia on 18 January 1939. While he didn't see active service, he dutifully undertook the oath, knowing full well its implications:

> I will well and truly serve our sovereign lord the King in the Militia Forces of the Commonwealth of Australia for the term of three years or until sooner lawfully discharged or removed, and that I will resist His Majesty's enemies and cause His Majesty's peace to be kept and maintained and that I will in all matters appertaining to my service faithfully discharge my duty according to the law.

Leo Fink, reservist number 324239 stood ready to protect the Australian homeland. Leo remained a member of the reserve army until he was discharged in late 1943.[16]

The threat of bombing and invasion were very real and planning for civilian safety and possible evacuation were diligently copied from the British experience. Voluntary organisations such as the Salvation Army, the Red Cross and the St John Ambulance Brigade together with council authorities and the police all came under the ultimate command of the Australian Army. Women flocked to volunteer their services. By 1940 the Victorian branch of the Australian Comforts Fund had 22,000 members. The federal government quickly saw the potential raised by volunteer women and compiled a National Voluntary Register in each state. Women were placed on standby as 'comfort providers', home nurses and cooks.[17] Throughout 1940, Mina Fink undertook three first-aid training courses with St John Ambulance, an international self-funded charitable organisation dedicated to helping people in sickness, distress, suffering and danger, whose Melbourne branch was founded in 1883. Mina learned to provide first aid to the injured, execute air raid precautions and undertake home nursing. On 9 December 1940, Mina received the St John Ambulance medallion in recognition of having passed all the requisite examinations. Just as she had kept her high school diploma, Mina proudly kept these certificates and the medallion for the rest of her life, as well as the photo of her graduating class in which she proudly donned the starched, neatly pressed nurse's uniform and the nurse's cap, the universally recognised symbol of the profession. It appealed to her sense of order, attention to detail and professionalism. For Mina, things always had to be done properly and with propriety. It was important to her not only to offer assistance, but to do so as a fully trained healthcare professional, to be recognised as such and qualified to undertake responsibilities that dealt with human lives. Melbourne did not come under enemy attack, but Mina, like her husband, stood ready to serve.[18]

Rallies, Demonstrations, Days of Mourning

Melbourne's Jewish community held large public meetings and rallies that were crucial for supporting Australia's war effort and bolstering recruitment drives for the armed forces. They gave the community an overall sense of solidarity, standing shoulder to shoulder with their fellow Australians. The local Jewish press urged the community to back its support with hard cash. 'No money – no victory. We must back the attack!'

For Eastern European Jews, specific events were also held to share precious, often hard to come by information about the Jewish catastrophe unfolding in Europe. The Kadimah hosted Yiddish 'living newspaper' forums, regularly attended by 300 to 400 people, in which community leaders would share information not readily available in the general press, whatever could be obtained through personal contacts and the Jewish Telegraphic Agency, an international news agency and wire service founded in 1917 to serve Jewish community newspapers and media around the world.

Community leaders also pressured the government to publicly condemn Nazi atrocities. Following a mass rally on 11 July 1942 to protest against the murder of European Jewry a series of resolutions demanding that the Allied powers prioritise the victims of Nazism and hold the perpetrators accountable according to the rule of law, were forwarded to leaders of the Allied powers: Curtin, Churchill, Roosevelt and Stalin. The rabbis declared days of mourning and Fast Days as a public means of dealing with private grief and loss. On 13 December 1942 a major Fast Day was declared in response to the grim reality that now confronted world Jewry. 'Himmler's decree that the Jews of Poland must be exterminated by the end of the year has shocked the world and plunged Jewry into deepest grief', the *Jewish Herald* reported.[19]

Jews 'Here' Pledge to Wage Their Own War

For Melbourne's immigrant Jews, showing solidarity through public meetings, rallies, demonstrations and signed petitions simply wasn't enough. Jews living 'here' were determined to make a difference to their fellow Jews struggling to survive 'over there'. 'It was our one chance in a lifetime to help', Mina recalled late in life.[20] Without firing a single shot, they would wage their own war. It would be an unconventional war fought without an army, without soldiers, a war fought at a distance, a war that would focus on helping the victims rather than targeting the perpetrators. The survival of the Jewish world, the greatest victory of all, depended on it.

Lessons learnt in Eastern Europe had taught Jews like Leo and Mina that a war like this had to be fought on their terms. Self-help and self-reliance, Jews helping other Jews, was the only way to succeed. Just as they had done in the past, they would need to turn to their own resources. The unprecedented scale of the catastrophe, however, presented a number of challenges. The amount of aid required to save lives was unmatched in living memory. This meant that an organisation had to be built that would bring the community together under one major relief fund, shift the fundraising focus away from competing domestic issues and raise extraordinary amounts of money and material goods. Managing and directing its distribution overseas, ensuring it got into the hands of those who desperately needed it, would require the involvement of world Jewry, a global network of well organised, experienced Jewish relief agencies. Above all it required visionary and imaginative leadership. Strong unwavering leadership.

Leo Makes His Move

By October 1942, Leo was making a name for himself as a community leader. As treasurer of the Kadimah, he proved himself to be a highly successful fundraiser, businessman and organiser – the annual bazaar, the Kadimah's main funding event, netted 50 per cent more than the previous year, all of which was distributed to different organisations supporting the war effort: the Red Cross; the Magen David Adom; the *Red Shield of David*, a medical relief agency formed in Tel Aviv in 1930 with subsequent branches in Haifa and Jerusalem; and the Russian Red Cross, a humanitarian aid society initiated by Czar Alexander II, in 1867. In addition, £220 was raised for the Australian Fighting Forces. This exceeded all previous amounts.[21]

Leo's communal leadership may have begun with the Kadimah but he moved quickly to embrace a vastly broader brief. When the Victorian United Emergency Committee (UEC) was formed on 21 January 1943, Leo was not on the executive. The UEC's main objective appeared to be public relations, bringing to the attention of the Australian public the extermination of Europe's Jews and to urge the repeal of the British 1939 White Paper which restricted entry of survivors to Palestine. There appears to be very little in the way of practical assistance to help survivors.[22] Leo, on the other hand, was planning a bolder, more expansive initiative with greater tangible outcomes. On 13 June 1943 a meeting was held to launch the Jewish People's Relief Fund (JPRF). An undated handbill, printed by York Press for the JPRF, stated its aim to be united with the struggles of the Jewish world, in keeping with Leo's own world view, one that emphasised the 'we' over the 'me':

To the Jewish People of Victoria …

We address this appeal to you in the most tragic time of our two-thousand-year-old martyrdom … Europe has become one huge slaughterhouse full of the innocent blood of our brothers and sisters … our brethren in the Ghetto of Warsaw … saw no other way out of their plight than armed resistance … although they knew well that they will pay for it with their lives … we Jews in Australia must do something too … should we remain inactive we shall never be forgiven by them … we must create a big JEWISH PEOPLE'S RELIEF FUND TO WHICH EVERY JEW SHOULD MAKE REGULAR CONTRIBUTIONS … we dare not think in terms of charity … but of the fulfilment of a great duty towards the whole of the Jewish people … stretch out a helping hand to your tortured kith and kin.[23]

A United Relief Fund Takes Shape

On 20 June 1943, Leo was elected president of the JPRF, unopposed, together with 25 board members, largely Eastern European Jewish immigrants who shared a similar world view. A delegation of three, including Leo, was elected to meet with the Victorian United Emergency Committee (UEC). While a merger was on the agenda it was really a takeover that was in the offing. With an eye always on the big picture, Leo didn't need rival groups acting as a distraction, best to bring them into the fold. Leo positioned himself to be the head of a strategic relief organisation with networks across the Jewish world.[24] At the same time, the women formed their own subgroup, a 'Ladies' Group' within the organisation. Mina was one of those charged with its establishment. The fund became the United Jewish Relief Fund in anticipation of the 'merger' with the UEC.[25] The *Australian Jewish News* on 23 July 1943 announced that 'full agreement has now been reached on a number of differences ... there will henceforth be one fund only to be known as the United Jewish Relief Fund (UJRF)'.

Membership subscriptions formed the basis of fundraising, with the ambitious aim that every Jewish household would become a contributor to the fund. By the outbreak of war there were some 10,000 Jews in Victoria, equating to approximately 2500 households. Leo knew that he would need to count on every family's contribution, either through membership or direct donation. It would require cooperation with the Jewish press for sustained publicity and the good will of every sector of the community.

But the UJRF still needed to negotiate the means by which funds and goods could be distributed overseas. Leo knew that for his work to succeed it had to be part of a much greater international Jewish relief network with offices in neutral and unoccupied countries and with the ability to enter military zones, provide food and shelter and render medical assistance. By late July 1943, UJRF had contacted the American Jewish Joint Distribution Committee (the Joint), established in 1914 and the largest international Jewish relief agency at the time; the Rescue Department of the Jewish Agency, a Zionist organisation founded in 1929; the Jewish Labour Committee in America, a secular organisation founded in 1934 by Yiddish-speaking immigrants in response to the threat posed by Nazism; and the World Jewish Congress founded in Geneva in August 1936 as an international federation of Jewish communities and organizations that would act as 'the diplomatic arm of the Jewish people'.[26]

At a meeting on 18 August 1943, Leo steered the UJRF towards a number of crucial internal business and management issues: tax deductibility to encourage donations and the move towards formalisation of the Ladies' Group, which occurred soon after on 26 September 1943.

Mina was immediately put on its executive. The UJRF also made contact with Jews in Shepparton, various Victorian country towns and Adelaide. By war's end it would also have a branch in Perth. Within three months of its inception, the UJRF membership stood at 454 pledges totalling £6650, with £2100 paid. Donations totalled £937. The UJRF minutes clearly outlined its main objective – to save Jewish lives through direct intervention: 'We advise the Jewish Agency that we await their detailed reports and that we emphasise that our aims are to help in rescuing European Jewry ... While money cannot yet be sent, goods can ... [we are] setting up a committee for collecting clothing, food etc'.[27] It was in the collection and handling of goods that Mina and her 'Ladies' Group' would make their mark.

To reflect more accurately its objective, on 7 October 1943, UJRF'S name was expanded to the United Jewish Overseas Relief Fund (UJORF), emphasising its intended global outreach while retaining a unity of purpose. This was no empty gesture or superficial label. The UJORF's charter was 'to render moral and financial support to European Jews wherever they may be'.[28] It also underpinned the way Leo perceived such an organisation had to operate in order to be effective, by positioning it on an international platform.

In October 1943, Leo also took on the presidency of the Kadimah, a position he held for just over six months and would ensure its 500 members would be on board with the UJORF. His message in the Kadimah's annual report clearly mirrored the UJORF's in stressing the need for unity amongst all Jews and the importance of Jewish continuity:

> The Nazi beasts have determined to wipe out the spirit of Jewish
> culture ... while we mourn for the loss of millions of Jews, we
> hold unshakeably that Jewry will continue to live [and] will be

reborn anew … We will do all in our power to enable those Jews who are left in Europe to take up their normal, healthy way of life again, and in so doing we will be doing all we can for the perpetuation of our own modern culture.[29]

While Leo retained an association with the Kadimah for the rest of his life, its cultural interests and its Yiddish centrality would always remain close to his heart, his immediate future was tied up with the urgency of providing relief and rescue.

Raising Funds and Controlling Their Distribution

At an extraordinary general meeting on 21 November, with 400 in attendance, the UJORF finalised its Constitution. Leo was again elected president on 9 December 1943. By the year's end, £5500 in funds were available. The amount of £3000 was immediately sent to the Joint for distribution at its discretion for relief of Jews seeking sanctuary in the neutral countries of Spain, Portugal, Switzerland and Sweden. A further £1500 was set aside for Russian Jews, with £1000 reserved for fares for those able to enter Palestine.

At the beginning of 1944, the UJORF announced ambitious plans to launch an appeal in June targeting another £50,000. This was the largest fundraising target ever set by an Australian Jewish organisation at the time. In today's currency £50,000 equates to A$3,600,000. This was an extraordinary amount given the size of the community and the war time conditions under which it was forced to operate.[30]

As funds continued to be raised and alliances were forged with international organisations, the UJORF's status grew. It now became important to control how and to whom the funds were dispersed. Leo ensured that the UJORF reserved the right to dictate the purposes for which funds were to be given, exercising fiscal control over the organisation and its overseas recipients. What was most important was that the funds went directly to those in need and were not to be absorbed in administrative expenses incurred by other agencies. There would be ongoing tensions between overseas agencies and the UJORF in how funds were used and distributed. This wasn't the only tension that Leo had to resolve.

Although a committed Zionist, Leo's communal work was always bipartisan. In what was a perceived power struggle between a powerful Zionist lobby and a strong band of Bundists within the UJORF, Leo sought to hose down an internal squabble by addressing concerns through an open letter to the *Australian Jewish News* on 8 December 1944. He clearly laid out the aims and objectives of the UJORF; that it was non-political and only acted in the interests of alleviating the suffering of Jews in Europe. 'Our aim is the relief and rescue of the Jewish individual unconditionally, irrespective of his world outlook or future plans.' His attack on factional interests proved productive. The UJORF did not splinter into supporting one group over another. It remained united with the sole purpose of providing aid to those most in need.

On 22 December 1944, in response to a lack of advice from the Jewish Agency over how they were distributing funds, Leo again asserted the UJORF's control over the distribution of funds, insisting they be used for 'relief and rescue work' and disallowing expenditure on administrative costs. In a demonstration of his single-minded approach to funding, Leo again requested more details from the Jewish Agency on its expenditure or risk cutting it off as a UJORF recipient. The UJORF received a cable on 12 February 1945 providing a breakdown of its expenses and advising that in order to send survivors to Palestine, the cost of £100 per person was required for transportation and maintenance.

To ensure control over expenditure was stringently adhered to, Mina suggested that funds be sent directly to Jews in liberated countries whenever possible. A decision was made to support specific projects at UJORF's discretion rather than give undirected funds to large organisations that were unable to guarantee exactly who received their funds or their method of distribution.[31]

By early 1945, the UJORF executive recommended that £10,000 be spent specifically on food and clothing for liberated Polish Jewry. It set an ambitious target of another £50,000 for its next appeal. The difficulty of raising such an amount was compounded by the number of different organisations seeking donations – every synagogue raised its own funds, Women's International Zionist Organization (WIZO), Judean Red Cross, Youth Aliya Committee, Jewish Philanthropic Society, the War Effort Circle, the Council of Jewish Women, Ezra Association, to name a few. All targeted the same families, the same individuals. All asked to dig deep and give generously.

Aid of a Different Nature

Buoyed by their success with raising funds and its effective control over distribution, the UJORF became bolder in its plans and aspirations. Dr Irving Weyman, a Jewish refugee doctor with Italian qualifications who arrived in Australia in 1939, moved that a Jewish medical mission to Europe be formed under the auspices of the UJORF, so that Jewish survivors could be aided by other Jews from around the world. It was thought that this would provide an important morale boost, demonstrating to survivors that the Jewish world was committed to their rehabilitation and to Jewish continuity.

Again, such a mission was an ambitious task given the number of approvals required from Australian and overseas agencies to get such a group off the ground, finding the resources, the necessary funding, the volunteers with the skills to staff it and the means of transporting the team to Europe. Passports were difficult to obtain as the Australian Government did not allow Australian technical personnel to leave the Commonwealth on relief work. This was eventually renegotiated successfully on humanitarian grounds. While the mission was formed and did arrive in Greece in the early months following liberation, its deployment was limited due to difficulties dealing with the United Nations Relief and Rehabilitation Administration (UNRRA), an international relief agency, founded in 1943 and largely dominated by the United States but representing 44 nations. The medical mission's formation was nevertheless testament to UJORF's tenacity and vision.[32]

The Work of Mina's 'Ladies' Group'

On 3 October 1944, Mina was elected president of the Ladies' Group, an auxiliary of the UJORF that she had helped to establish and organise. By now the 'Ladies' Group' was in charge of a large, industrious network operating out of workrooms located at 22 Patrick Street, in a warehouse tucked away in a dark building halfway along a small laneway in Melbourne's CBD. Mina would always refer proudly to these 900 volunteers as 'her army', women who worked tirelessly at the task at hand; collecting, sorting, cleaning, mending and packing tons of clothing and blankets. In describing the work of the 'relief fund Ladies' Group' a journalist for the Jewish press spent a day with the volunteers.

> A band of women working seven hours a day, six days a week doing a job whose value can scarcely be estimated in words … the first impression is one of a smoothly running and perfectly functioning organisation … garments are sorted, sent to the

cleaners, shoes are repaired, clothes that are torn or unsuitable … are mended and altered … then classed according to whether they are suitable for summer or winter, children or adults, male or female … then packed in crates awaiting shipment.[33]

Collection depots were established: four in Carlton, two in Caulfield, two in St Kilda, two in Kew and three in Armadale. The Jewish press urged citizens to 'share their own clothing and food with your unfortunate brethren overseas. They have given their all so that you can survive'.

Mina's organisational leadership and expertise were evident in the efficiency of the entire process and in her insistence that any goods sent to those in need was of a high standard. Charity with dignity was her mantra. Those in need were to be treated with respect. Leo also highlighted the work of the Ladies' Group in a published letter in the *Australian Jewish News* on 8 December 1944. 'They are responsible for every article from an overcoat to a vest, from the time it leaves a Jewish home in Australia until the time it reaches a Jewish home in some far corner of the world.'

Mina established a comprehensive, broad range of fundraising activities, activated through six major subgroups across the entire metropolitan area, each with its own group leader. Recitals and concerts, garden fetes, luncheons, raffles, collections and cash donations, grand balls, a gift shop in a basement at 100 Bourke Street, functions held at life cycle events, all had proceeds going to the UJORF. Her plans for future growth included promoting an active Youth Group, which became operational in 1944. No stone was left unturned. No opportunity was missed.

On 13 April 1945, Mina's Ladies' Group announced its biggest clothing shipment overseas: 'The Relief Fund shipped 93 cases (20,000 pounds) of clothing to liberated Jews in Poland'. Again, this took considerable engineering and negotiation. The country was still on a war footing and shipping was difficult to obtain. Government approval was sought and obtained.[34] One month later, Mina again demonstrated her fundraising prowess, presenting a cheque for £5000 to the UJORF. The Ladies' Group optimistically reported that, 'She hopes to present a similar cheque again before end of year', which she did.[35]

Mina's great strength was in her ability to draw others along with her. Inspired by her energy, efficiency and enthusiasm, her volunteers often became lifelong friends and loyal co-workers. Late in life, one such friend reminded Mina that 'I joined the organisation because of you. I did what I did because of you'. It was a leadership style that would again come to the fore decades later.[36]

Liberation. What Did It Mean?

From June 1944, pockets of Europe were being liberated, but the task of liberating the entire European continent would take another 11 months. It was not until May 1945 that Europe was fully freed from Nazi oppression. But liberation meant different things to different people. Ticker-tape parades welcomed home the victors. There were celebrations and joyful reunions. The leaders of the free world promised a new world order. But the end of hostilities did not bring the end of suffering to the Jewish survivors. Homeless and destitute, many were unrepatriable, unwilling and unable to return to their former homes and former lives. They desperately needed help to rebuild their lives and start afresh.

In the UJORF's first annual general meeting report, issued on 30 June 1944, Leo understood that the community's commitment to survivors would require a mighty, concerted effort:

> When Europe is finally freed, the remnants of European Jewry will present a ghastly picture of havoc and utter misery. They can be helped only by a concerted and sustained effort of their fellow Jews in the free countries. In this global effort of world Jewry, we Jews of Australia will have to play a part that far outweighs our numerical strength.

In the same report Leo noted the organisation's considerable achievements. In just over 12 months since its inception, the UJORF had allocated £40,100 to Jewish relief organisations overseas. Membership of the UJORF had risen to 1794 and that of the Ladies' Group to 771. Another £18,000 had been collected, with £7000 remitted to the Joint in Jerusalem and £750 to the work of the Jewish Labour Committee in America.[37]

By June 1945 the UJORF reported that 18 tons of honey, 22 tons of soap, 26,000 woollen blankets, 1500lbs of kosher meat, over 20,000 items of clothing, 6800 pairs of shoes, copious quantities of tinned food and sheepskins had been donated, or purchased, and shipped overseas. Wartime exigencies had prevented the purchase and shipment of other supplies still under ration, such as condensed milk and dried egg powder. Another £42,000 had been sent to relief agencies overseas.[38]

The UJORF Shifts Direction

The new emerging crisis confronting European Jewry was how to survive survival? In response, the UJORF began a tracing service to connect survivors with Melbourne relatives, indicating an important shift in direction from relief towards rescue and resettlement. In moving their work from saving victims to actions that would rescue and reunite survivors with living relatives in Melbourne, the UJORF began publishing and disseminating lists of survivors.

On 27 April 1945 a survivors' list from Theresienstadt arrived at the UJORF office and by the end of June 1945, David Abzac, a steadfast UJORF volunteer, undertook to publish all survivor lists and distribute 40 copies to different organisations for inspection. By war's end over 75,000 names on 1200 printed pages were received and forwarded. Soon the UJORF office was inundated with requests from local Jews for assistance in locating any family survivors in Europe. Once family members were located, individuals in the community could use the parcel service set up by the UJORF to send them food and clothing. Over a thousand local enquiries were received in the office and searches were undertaken by European organisations tasked with handling the urgent work of reuniting fractured families. While the UJORF office acted as an intermediary, the workload became so intense that the UJORF had to deploy a full-time member of its office staff to just handle the enquiries, both from overseas and locally. The following excerpt from a contemporary report written by a UJORF Board member A Shulman, 'A Half-Hour in the Office of the United Overseas Relief Fund' details some of the emotional scenes that happened there on a daily basis.

> We see a lady from Vienna, who is hurriedly asking questions, with her characteristic German-English accent. She is anxious to see lists of liberated Jews from Theresienstadt. Her parents were last heard of there … Close by stands a Hungarian Jew. He wants the lists of survivors from Belsen. Joyfully he exclaims as he sees his brother's name; but unfortunately, there are no details. The Secretary of the Fund promises him to find out the best and speediest method of communicating with his brother. A Polish Jew nervously peruses the pages, and repeats, under his breath, several names – as if afraid to forget them. He lingers over each name on the closely typed pages … a young man comes in and

addresses himself to the clerk. Last week's paper stated that a letter was received by the office addressed to him. The clerk promptly hands the letter over to him. It is a postcard from the Belsen camp. The young man is profuse in his thanks and goes over to the furthest corner to read it. He looks at it for a minute or two, and hangs his head: another moment and his shoulders are shaking with suppressed sobs. The four walls of the office bear silent witness to a scene oft repeated in thousands of Jewish homes all over the world.[39]

The UJORF initially decided to leave immigration matters to the Jewish Welfare and Polish Immigration Society. But by September 1945, the UJORF had changed its policy on immigration, prompted by the plight of Jews stranded in Shanghai during the war and now wanting to come to Australia. It was the frustrating lack of immediate progress on the matter that spurred them on to take action. From then on, the UJORF became a prime mover in immigration and resettlement.[40]

Leo's UJORF President's 'Victory Year 1945' report highlighted the need for a new direction: 'Continuous relief only cannot solve the problem of becoming independent and self-supporting. We must endeavour to rehabilitate [survivors] and do everything in our power to take them out from camp collectivism and regimentation to individual initiative and independence'.

By the war's end, and within two short years, the UJORF was the largest and strongest Jewish organisation in Australia, with 2310 active members. Leo and Mina had built an expansive grassroots movement and connected it with a worldwide Jewish network.

Leo and Mina had set out to give practical aid and relief to Jewish victims of genocide. Unprecedented funds were raised, relief was delivered, lives were saved. A world was rescued. As Rabbi Wyshkowsky observed, 'It is the only institution in the history of Australian Jewry that has brought together every strata of the Jewish community, all with the one unified purpose – that is, the saving of their fellow Jews'.[41] But Leo and Mina's work was far from over. Their biggest challenge still lay ahead. It would require all their ingenuity, leadership skills and bravado. Rebuilding the lives of thousands of survivors would depend on it.

Chapter 7

'A WELCOME,
A JOB, A HOME
AND A FUTURE'

Max Zilberman never forgot the day he arrived in Melbourne. And he never forgot the person who was waiting to meet him.

> We arrived at Spencer street station on the morning of 21 January 1949 where a lady with a big smile on her face introduced herself to us as Mrs Mina Fink. Other people from the Welfare Society were also there.[1]

Polish-born Max Zilberman, Buchenwald concentration camp survivor, had spent the first three post-war years in Switzerland, under the auspices of the Swiss Red Cross. He, and others, spent their time recuperating from years of starvation and abuse, slowly learning to live again. They worked, learnt a trade or attended school. But it was clear that their time in Switzerland was temporary. They knew that they would have to find a permanent place to call home. Returning to Poland was not an option for Max. There was nothing to return to.

In 1948, the recently reconstituted Australian Jewish Welfare and Relief Society, now under the leadership of Leo Fink, offered to sponsor Max, who was living in Geneva at the time, and a number of other young male survivors from his group, to resettle in Melbourne. Not knowing much about this far-flung continent, Max managed to get hold of a Swiss edition of *Reader's Digest* which featured an article about Australia. The lure of beautiful sunny beaches and young pretty girls was more than enough to entice the young man, keen for a fresh start in a new, promising land. 'I and many others jumped at the chance to come here and finally in 1948 in the port of Marseille we boarded the *Eridan* bound for Australia.'[2] The *Eridan*, a French passenger ship built in 1928, had its own colourful history. The outbreak of war saw the vessel, docked in Marseille, come under the control of the Vichy government. In 1942 the US captured the ship and sent it to Britain for conversion into a troopship carrier with a capacity of 1200. The post-war period saw it undergo its third incarnation into a migrant ship, one of many that would transport refugees and immigrants to a new life in a new land, before it was taken out of service in 1956.[3]

Max departed Marseille on 23 November 1948. The ship, once described as France's largest modern 'motor ship' with state-of-the-art facilities, including a lavish dining saloon and 'smoking' room, had clearly seen better times. Onboard life was described as a 'horrible nightmare' with 'indescribable filthy conditions'. Meagre rations, unpalatable food, poor sanitation and overcrowded, squalid living quarters led to the passengers reporting the ship to the press as a floating 'pigsty'. When the *Eridan* left Marseille on its 60-day journey to Sydney via Panama and Tahiti, it carried 761 passengers of 17 different nationalities, well in excess of its 315 capacity. By the time it docked in Sydney on 19 January 1949, 233 passengers had already disembarked at other ports. Max was one of its remaining 528 passengers.[4]

The appalling state of many of these migrant ships remained a sore point. On 27 May 1949, in a letter to Lewis Neikrug, secretary of the Hebrew Immigrant Aid Society (HIAS) based in Paris, Leo voiced concern over extremely overcrowded and filthy conditions on boats such as the *Ville d'Amiens* and *Luciano Manara*. These migrant ships continually received adverse publicity, with Jewish passengers shouldering the blame for the appalling conditions. The newspapers also pointed to the poor health of many migrants, implying that they were deliberately being slipped through the medical check-ups. Leo instructed Neikrug to tighten up the process as it jeopardised the whole migration program. Too much was at stake.[5]

Whatever the circumstances surrounding Max Zilberman's own passage, he quickly put the travails of the journey behind him. He was met at the wharf by Jewish Welfare workers, given overnight accommodation, then boarded the train for Melbourne where Mina awaited his arrival. Max, like so many other Holocaust survivors, was glad to 'be leaving the cursed continent of Europe behind', glad to leave behind a shattered, broken graveyard continent, filled with nothing but the dust and ashes of a lost world.[6]

The Task of Resettlement

What Max and other new arrivals didn't know when they first set foot on Australian soil was the monumental effort undertaken by Jewish individuals such as Leo and Mina Fink, the organisations they led and the army of volunteers who worked with them, that enabled survivors like himself to start a new life in Australia. Chapter 1 describes in detail the government hurdles that had to be jumped in order to secure passage and landing permits for Jewish immigrants. While post-war Australia embarked on an expansive nation building exercise which required growing the population through migration, Jewish immigration was not part of the big picture. The government's position was reinforced by an Australian press and a xenophobic population that was hostile to and suspicious and fearful of large numbers of 'foreigners' arriving on their shores.[7]

While the Australian Government did allow the admission of Jews, it washed its hands of any further involvement, refusing to provide any financial support to Jewish immigration and resettlement, in stark contrast to the incentives extended to other migration programs.

Responsibility and cost for the reception and integration of all Jewish immigrants would have to be borne by Australian Jewry. The local Jewish community had to rely on their own resources. Again, it would fall to Jews helping other Jews. Once more they would need to muster the considerable financial and material support needed, but this time their responsibility was far greater, stretching the limits of this small community. At the same time, another demand on Jewish resources emerged in the form of the newly established State of Israel. Amidst all of this, and in spite of the challenges it posed, Melbourne would become home to one of the largest Holocaust survivor communities in the world. And it is here that another side of Leo and Mina's epic story lies.

Meeting the Boats

By the end of 1947, Jewish immigrants were arriving in large numbers. It was the end of one journey and the start of another. Max remembered the first step of his Australian journey. 'We got into their cars and they took us to the Welfare Society home in Burke Road, Camberwell where we met many of our friends who had arrived a few weeks earlier'.[8]

From the moment the new arrivals stepped ashore the hands-on work really began. Leo and Mina played their part, not just as team leaders but as dedicated team members ready to roll up their sleeves and do whatever needed to be done. Committees were set up to meet the new arrivals at the dock, act as translators, usher them through customs, take them to their next destination and provide care and support if they were in transit. An excerpt from the *Australian Jewish Herald* detailed the arrangements that had to be put in place to welcome those on the SS *Tidewater* when it docked in Melbourne on 13 November 1947 at 8am. While only one example, it illustrates the sort of unrelenting work that was required from the moment the Jewish Welfare volunteers met the new arrivals. Additional volunteers and resources from other organisations were called upon to share the load. Mina Fink and the indefatigable David Abzac played key roles in the overall organisation of the program.

> The landing arrangements and customs clearances were well planned and most of the 56 passengers who disembarked in Melbourne left the dock within three hours. Jewish Welfare and Relief Society officials helped and facilitated these arrangements, Mr D Abzac and Mr Fischer, both of whom had previously boarded the ship, interpreted for customs officials after the ship had entered the Bay.
>
> When the passengers began to come down the gangway ... the staff of the Relief and Welfare Society, under the leadership of Mr and Mrs L Fink, began their valuable work assisting those passengers bound for Sydney and other states. The National Council of Jewish Women led by Mrs R Simmons and the Council for Jewish Immigrants represented by Mr F R Benfrey, helped to maintain a shuttle service of private cars between Victoria Dock and the Kadimah in Carlton where lunch had been prepared for those passengers who were proceeding to other states.[9]

The memory of Mina's 'big smile' greeting him never left Max, but for Mina, the task of meeting and greeting new arrivals was often confronting as many Holocaust survivors were understandably distrustful of strangers. 'I remember how I used to come home and cry at their reaction to me. They used to look at me with suspicion, thinking "what does she want from us?" I felt that they did not trust me. This was not to be wondered at, after all they had been through.'[10]

Mina put her personal feelings aside to deal with the formidable task at hand. 'Since 1946', one record revealed, '500 ships and planes, carrying 10,500 persons including 3000 children arrived in Melbourne and were met on their arrival by the Australian Jewish Welfare and Relief Society.'[11]

A Bold Vision

Leo Fink's vision was to advance Australian Jewry. As he saw it, new arrivals, like Max Zilberman, would serve a dual purpose. Holocaust survivors, desperate to start life afresh would be given an opportunity to rebuild their lives in a safe, secure and bountiful country, a country that had enabled his own family to prosper and thrive. At the same time the local Jewish community would be bolstered, not only by the sheer weight of increased numbers, but through cultural enrichment and greater diversity. While the increase in Jewish numbers would never reach the same density of pre-war cities such as the Finks' Bialystok, and the Australian Jewish population would never exceed a half of 1 per cent of the total population, increased numbers would shore up a small and potentially vulnerable community, a community threatened not by antisemitism but by assimilation and intermarriage. By developing the Australian Jewish community, Leo and Mina believed that the Jewish world, the world to which they were so closely connected, would also be strengthened. At its core were the perennial issues of survival and continuity.

Israel versus Australia

The issue of survival raised another matter that would test the local community's resolve. On 2 December 1947, the United Jewish Overseas Relief Fund (UJORF) sent a congratulatory telegram to the Jewish Agency concerning the 'UN decision to establish a Jewish State in Palestine'.[12] Amidst the euphoria and celebrations of the State of Israel's Declaration of Independence on 14 May 1948, another debate quickly emerged over the type of support that the fledgling State should be given. Where should Jewish survivors be resettled? Shouldn't they be sent to defend and develop the new State? Shouldn't they be directed away from Australia?[13] These questions preoccupied Jewish relief agencies, Jewish governing bodies, here and abroad.

For some survivors, like Max, the first priority was just being able to leave Europe, getting 'away from all the bad memories', although he acknowledged that 'many wanted to go to Israel', hoping to build a new life while also building a new Jewish State.[14] Clearly this debate presented an ideological struggle for a community deeply committed to Jewish survival both 'here' and 'there'.

To a large extent the matter was resolved at an executive level in February 1949 at a special immigration conference in Melbourne. Paul Morawetz, honorary secretary of the Executive Council of Australian Jewry (ECAJ), a peak body for the state-based representative bodies that was created in 1944, prosecuted the case in favour of immigration to Israel. Paul had visited Europe in November 1948 and attended an American Jewish Joint Distribution Committee (the Joint) conference in Paris. Having directly witnessed the obstacles imposed by Australian authorities in trying to discourage, suppress and slow down Jewish immigration, he became convinced that Australian Jewry should not sponsor Jewish migration here, but rather shore up support for the newly established State of Israel and focus its resources to that end. There was heated debate but the motion was defeated and the ECAJ, with Leo Fink in solid agreement as chairman of the ECAJ Immigration Committee, stated that while immigration to Israel should take priority, those Jews who wished to migrate to Australia should still be assisted by bodies such as the ECAJ and Jewish Welfare. Morawetz resigned as a result of this decision.[15]

Of particular concern was the way that this conflict of loyalties redirected fundraising priorities. A new sense of urgency emerged. Israel presented a new challenge with its own pressing needs. If the war taught many in the Australian Jewish community one thing, it was that building a Jewish homeland, a place where Jews could find sanctuary, was paramount. The Zionist fundraising appeal in 1948, at the time of Israel's War of Independence, was a wake-up call to those invested in bringing survivors to Melbourne. It raised £150,000 for the newly established Jewish State while the Jewish Welfare Appeal, dealing with domestic matters, raised only £25,614.

UJORF and Jewish Welfare Join Forces under Leo's Leadership

During the war years, Jewish survival meant that fundraising to support Jews caught in the hellfire of the Holocaust was the community's immediate concern. But the need to support local Jews suffering hardship continued unabated. Jewish philanthropy in Melbourne dates back to the Jewish Congregational Society formed in 1841.[16] The Australian Jewish Welfare Society (AJWS), a philanthropic organisation that underwent a number of name changes in the 1930s before it became the AJWS in 1938, focused on a range of local welfare services to the migrant community at this time. The Larino children's home, agricultural resettlement, subsistence loans for those experiencing hardships and the Polish Youth Migrant Fund all continued to receive assistance. With a shift in the UJORF's direction from relief to resettlement in the immediate post-war years, the UJORF needed to refocus its efforts on the domestic matters of absorption and integration. Having two organisations overlapping in their operations and competing for funds was counterproductive, confusing and costly. Streamlining the two organisations into one structure made good sense. It was a process that required considerable administrative restructuring. It was complicated. Steps were needed to put everything in place. Leo began by expanding his influence on two key organisations. In July 1946, he placed UJORF representatives on both the Victorian Jewish Advisory Board and the AJWS.[17]

In August 1946, Isaac Boas, a respected leader of the Anglo Jewish establishment, resigned as chairman of the Australian Jewish Welfare Society (AJWS) and Alec Masel, the inaugural president of the Executive Council of Australian Jewry, temporarily stepped in with an understanding that Leo, with whom he had a sound working relationship, would 'help to adjust the position in the Office'[18] Masel, born in Fremantle to Russian Jewish immigrants, a successful practising Melbourne lawyer and influential power broker, was keen for the energetic, visionary Leo to come on board and enfold the AJWS into the operations of the UJORF. In the following two months, there were discussions to merge the UJORF and AJWS into one organisation within an 18-month to two-year transition period. Leo would sit at the helm of both organisations until the new entity emerged.

Procedures moved rapidly. On 9 September 1946 Leo informed the UJORF Board that it was now the sole organisation dealing with 'emigration arrangements'. By December 1946, Leo effectively ran both the AJWS and UJORF.

On 1 July 1947 the Australian Jewish Welfare and Relief Society (AJWRS) as it was renamed to incorporate the broader 'relief' operations now at its core, held its first meeting as the result of the two amalgamated organisations, although the AJWRS as a fully constituted body in its own right, would not hold its first AGM until November 1948, by which time the UJORF would be formally wound up. While this would be hailed as a merger, in fact it brought into existence an entirely new organisation with a broad and powerful mandate. By 23 February 1948, Leo's growing authority was further recognised. He was elected to the Executive of the Victorian Jewish Board of Deputies.

Nevertheless, by 20 July 1948, the Australian Jewish Welfare and Relief Society (AJWRS) was already acting with its own authority. In a bold initiative, the AJWRS negotiated for and received federal government assurance that it could act as a 'corporate' sponsor for individuals without family or friends to support their application. Under Leo, the AJWRS took on a 'blanket guarantee' scheme to take over all responsibilities concerning migrants, including the issuing of permits, as it had done for Max Zilberman.[19] Over 8000 landing permits were applied for by the AJWRS in the first four years of the scheme's operation.[20] Leo noted his success with government negotiations in a personal letter to Lewis Neikrug on 4 March 1949; 'By now you have most likely received from the Executive Council a report of our deliberations, and you can guess that I have taken a lion's share in bringing about a change in the Government's policy'.[21]

This 'blanket guarantee' involved ensuring that all immigrants would not be a burden on the State for five years. The AJWRS would act in the place of a personal guarantor, help to secure employment, provide accommodation for a minimum of six months, support welfare needs, extend loans and provide access to medical assistance. For local Jews who could act as personal guarantor for family or friends, the AJWRS acted as go between, often liaising between the different parties. Between November 1947 and March 1948, the Migration Committee of the AJWRS dealt with 2000 letters, interviewed 92 applicants as guarantors, and opened 472 new cases involving 626 migrants. It had also handled over £21,000 in deposits and full payments for fares.

The AJWRS migration report of 28 September 1948 revealed its staggering achievements: 'Those assisted by AJWS and UJORF between 1 Jan 1947 and 31 August 1948 totalled 2086. The total Jewish population of Melbourne was 14,231. A number of these arrivals would have been included in that figure so the increase that the community had to cope with was close to 20 per cent in a period of just over 18 months'.

The report from the newly constituted AJWRS first annual general meeting on 15 November 1948 (covering an 18-month period from mid-1947 to 1948) revealed the breadth of its activities: migration, transportation, reception, housing, employment, loans and sustenance, medical care, children's care, overseas relief and searches for missing relatives, English classes, and fundraising. Their coordination required endless meetings, discussions and resolutions, reflecting Leo's own democratic and inclusive leadership style. Some 200 board meetings alone were held in that one year.[22] On average this translated into numerous additional meetings, often more than three to four per week, in addition to all the work those meetings and their subcommittees generated. But it was the vigorous work of the collective, the work that every member of the organisation undertook that Mina remembered with pride. 'We worked with tremendous energy. I have never encountered such devotion in any other organisation since.'[23]

In 1948, Mina's influence as an executive of the AJWRS broadened. She requested and received greater autonomy from the AJWRS Board in decision making. The welfare of children was a recurring concern for Mina, in particular the resettlement of child survivors and vulnerable local children in care. Mina's 'Ladies' Group' successfully sponsored 97 orphaned children under the auspices of the OSE Central Board in Geneva, and found them Jewish homes with Melbourne parents. Mina had direct involvement in the care of children at the Larino Home hostel, seeing that their education, medical and social needs were being met. Mina also took a personal interest in individual children in difficult circumstances, often showing initiative in resolving problematic cases. Newly arrived mothers often needed to work while caring for their children. Mina sought and found places of employment where the mothers could take their children with them, or she arranged day care for children not of school age.

On 28 February 1949, Leo was re-elected chairman of AJWRS and Mina was unanimously re-elected chairperson of the AJWRS Ladies' Group.

Within a relatively short time frame the AJWRS became the foremost relief organisation dealing with every aspect of Holocaust survivor resettlement in the country. But it was only able to do so with the considerable support of important allies.

International Jewish Support

The power and might of an interconnected Jewish world had to be called upon once again. This time overseas Jewish aid organisations were asked to provide the financial backbone to Jewish resettlement 'down under'. Their support was critical. Transportation costs and accommodation were areas of greatest expenditure. In a directive penned to Walter Brand the secretary of Jewish Welfare in Sydney, Leo emphasised the seriousness of the matter. 'You might as well make it clear to Mr Newman [President, Executive Council of Australian Jewry] that we will not undertake anything beyond our means and without such funds from overseas our immigration possibilities will have to be drastically curtailed.'[24]

In the aftermath of the Holocaust and the obliteration of European Jewry, the balance of power had shifted away from Europe to the USA. In the post-war era American Jewry emerged as the largest, wealthiest and most powerful diasporic community in the world.

There is little doubt that without the financial assistance of the USA's three key Jewish relief agencies, the American Jewish Joint Distribution Committee (the Joint), the Hebrew Immigrant Aid Society (HIAS), the Refugee Economic Corporation (REC), the number of Jewish Holocaust survivors able to be resettled in Australia would have been dramatically reduced.[25] Following Leo Fink's own trip to Europe in early 1946 where he established close links with HIAS, Australia was visited by two representatives of the Joint, Gertrude van Tijin in December 1946, who successfully pleaded the case with Arthur Calwell for resettling stranded Shanghai Jews, and Charles Jordan in August/September 1947, the Joint's representative in Shanghai at the time, who also reported back on the needs of Australian Jewish welfare organisations. In describing the urgent plight of Jews stuck in Shanghai, Jordan lauded the efforts of Australian Jewry when he told the UJORF at a special meeting on 8 September, 'On a per capita basis Australian Jews have sent more relief than any other Jewish community in the world'.[26]

Most important of all was the visit of REC secretary and dignitary Emery Komlos in September 1949, who was charged with representing the Joint, HIAS and REC. In a crucial meeting between Jewish Welfare officials and Komlos, Leo stressed the importance of securing substantial external funding. 'We here are very interested in Jewish immigration and we have to turn to overseas organisations for assistance.' In striking a deal, Leo did not hesitate to impress upon Komlos the financial backing that Australia Jewry had previously given the Joint, HIAS and REC. Now was the time for some reciprocal support. 'I am trying to work out the value in money which we have contributed to the Joint, I think about half a million pounds, shiploads of soap, canned milk and other items', and 'as regards HIAS ... we got up a special committee to work out ways and means to press out of the Jewish community over £150,000 for the [cost of] transportation'.[27] Finally, Leo said 'If America will only realise that they will have to their credit for their few thousand pounds the establishment of a new community in a new continent, not only a new country'.[28] On his departure Komlos wrote an influential report that was instrumental in immediately securing US$200,000 to establish more hostels and extend personal loans to immigrants, equivalent to US$3,570,000 in purchasing power today. The Joint would provide $120,000, HIAS $40,000 and REC $40,000. Komlos praised the work undertaken by Australian Jewry, its leadership and its management of the resettlement program, '4000 Jews who come to Australia this year are finding exactly what they seek and what we want them to have: a welcome, a job, a home, and a future'.[29]

There would be many subsequent requests from the AJWRS for assistance, haggling over the amounts offered by the Joint, HIAS and REC and the terms agreed to, mostly with significant positive outcomes, until the Conference on Jewish Material Claims Against Germany (the Claims Conference) assumed responsibility for assisting Australian Jewry in 1954, by which time most of the Holocaust survivors who would immigrate to Australia had already done so.

Hostels, Jobs, Education

Within the first eight months of the post-war immigration period, over 50 per cent of Jewish arrivals came to Melbourne. In that short time, the community had to house and find employment for nearly 1000 new arrivals. By 1949 the problem had grown to an average of 3000 new arrivals per year with nearly 2000 of them settling in Melbourne.

The immediate problem confronting the newcomers and those charged with their absorption was securing guaranteed accommodation for a minimum period of six months, without which a landing permit would not be issued. This was exacerbated by an acute housing shortage that gripped Australia in the post-war years. In part this was due to the lack of housing construction during the Depression and the war years, and the problem only deepened with soaring post-war immigration. The 1947 census indicated that there were only 877 dwellings for every 1000 households Australia-wide. A 1949 Australian gallup poll found that one in four households was home to an extra family member or individual who would have lived separately if accommodation had been available.[30]

As increasing numbers of Jewish immigrants began to arrive, the need for temporary housing grew. Mina recalled the problem this posed and the solutions that were found.

The Australian Jewish Welfare had to guarantee housing because at that time housing was very difficult to obtain. Several shelters were established, one in Burke Road, another in Carlton, in Coburg and in St Kilda. People were brought into the shelters and some of them stayed for a period of six months or more until they were able to find a room, a boarding house or flat. At that time there were no professional staff, no social workers, only volunteers to care for them.[31]

Max fondly remembered his time in the Camberwell hostel and Mina's involvement. 'We stayed at this home for a while. Mrs Fink was almost a daily visitor, talking to us, giving advice, always with a friendly smile, helping us to get jobs or find accommodation.'[32]

The establishment of hostels to deal with growing numbers of immigrants and a shortage in housing was not unique to the Jewish community. Hostel accommodation was a common feature of urban life throughout Melbourne in the years following the Second World War. As part of its immigration policy the Commonwealth Government established a number of migrant hostels in suburbs such as Williamstown, Springvale and Nunawading. Hostels were also established by semi-government organisations such as the Victorian Railways, the Melbourne and Metropolitan Tramways Board and the State Electricity Commission. These places provided accommodation for thousands of mostly male immigrants employed in large-scale infrastructure projects.[33]

The establishment of privately managed Jewish hostels in Melbourne greatly aided the absorption of newly arrived Jewish immigrants. Jewish Welfare and the *landsmanshaftn*, self-help organisations set up by immigrants from the same geographic region, often worked hand in hand in the resettlement program. Many of their leaders were also directly involved with Jewish Welfare.

In January 1947, Leo successfully negotiated with the Bialystoker Centre, the oldest and most influential *landsmanshaft* in Melbourne, for temporary accommodation. By February 1947, UJORF and AJWS had a range of 'welcoming, housing and employment subcommittees' to deal with the most immediate issues. A hostel was purchased at 19 Robe Street in St Kilda in July 1947, the first of 11 properties purchased by AJWRS and the *landsmanshaftn* between 1947 and 1951, with three purchased in 1947 and four purchased in 1949. All hostels were bought either fully or in part with funds donated by overseas Jewish organisations, with the Joint being the major contributor.[34]

By February 1948, Mina and her Ladies' Group were running every aspect of Camberwell House, the largest of the hostels. 'I was put in charge of the Burke Road Camberwell hostel where the Buchenwald Boys resided.'[35] By November that year Mina's strong involvement with her 'Buchenwalders' saw her take responsibility for much of their welfare and education. The House report to the AJWRS recorded that:

> Mrs Fink informed the [AJWRS] Board that everything is done to make their stay a pleasant one, and every boy received £1 weekly pocket money. The House Committee had extra expenses for urgently needed clothing for the boys. Mrs Fink also arranged for the boys to attend English Classes at the Taylor's College as from Monday November 8. Dr Benfrey suggested that Taylor's College be requested to let this Society have weekly reports on the attendance of the boys.

When Mina heard that one of the boys wanted to further his studies, she personally undertook to find a private sponsor for him.[36]

At the same time, Mina was dealing with other urgent cases of financial need and asked that 'sustenance' procedures provided by the AJWRS be simplified and expedited. As a result, Mina was given greater autonomy to give up to £50 in urgent cases, a substantial amount at a time when the average weekly wage for a male factory worker was between £6 and £7.

Accommodation remained a major concern until the early 1950s by which time Jewish immigration had decreased considerably. On 25 May 1949, Leo wrote a letter to Mr Telsey at HIAS New York, explaining the resettlement challenge that still lay ahead: 'You are no doubt aware that Jewish immigration to Australia, which a few years ago was a matter of expediency, a matter of saving lives, is now becoming a problem of permanent settlement ... one of the greatest obstacles in absorbing immigrants in this country is the problem of accommodation'. Again, in a letter of 9 June 1949, to Henry Shoshkes at the HIAS office in New York, Leo again pressed the case of high immigration figures and the struggle to absorb them:

> Looking through recent figures, I see that the number of Jewish post-war arrivals in this country is very close to 7600 persons (not for publication please). You will agree that for a Jewish population of 30,000, this presents a very great task to absorb them, and especially as we expect to bring over to this country, by various ways and means in the next two or three years' time a good few thousand more.

At the same time Leo voiced his concerns at an Executive Council of Australian Jewry (ECAJ) two-day conference, held in Melbourne from 11 June to 13 June 1949, where he tabled his Immigration report, '3000 [Jewish] people will enter Australia during the year', he foreshadowed. 'The problem will be the absorption of the immigrants into the Australian Jewish community, not the obtaining of permits.'[37]

Finding work for the new arrivals was not, as Mina recalled, very difficult. 'In the years 1947–9 employment was not difficult to come by. Many who were trained as professionals had to work as labourers as their qualifications were not recognised.'[38] But work was plentiful, post-war recovery was well under way.

By the end of the 1940s, hostel accommodation had been provided to over 3000 immigrants, employment found for 1050 individuals, £13,500 given to the sick or unemployed as sustenance.[39]

A Special Bond

Mina's connection to Max Zilberman and the other 'Buchenwald Boys', went above and beyond organisational arrangements and commitments. It represented a special bond that was borne out of extraordinary circumstances. Mina recognised that she was 'particularly drawn to many of the younger people who arrived here'. Mina's affinity with the younger arrivals partly stemmed from her own youth, she was still only a 36-year-old woman in 1949, while her childhood years as an orphan enabled her to identify with the pain experienced by many younger survivors. While she had grandparents who cared for her, others were cast adrift without any support, alone in an unfamiliar world.

Max recalled the way in which Mina became an important part of their lives in those early resettlement years.

> I remember when I got injured at work Mina came to visit me together with Freda [her daughter] and they brought me goodies … On a personal level she invited some of us to visit the family in their holiday home in Frankston … on another occasion they would drive up and take some of us for a drive to the country for Sunday lunch. Everything was done in such a friendly manner, we always felt at ease with her. We really liked her very much, we felt that her concern for us was genuine and that she really cared. She affectionately called us 'the Buchenwald Boys' and our stay

at the Welfare home was the start of our friendship with Mrs Fink that would last for years.[40]

Max's close bond with the other 'Buchenwald Boys' and their enduring friendship with Mina Fink would span decades, until her death in 1990. 'We slowly started to get married … the honoured guests were always Mina and Leo Fink'. Leo and Mina often performed the symbolic act of being 'unterfirers' (a Yiddish word meaning those who accompany the bride or groom during the marriage ceremony), at many of their weddings. As they walked the groom down the aisle and stood behind him under the wedding canopy, they represented the young man's missing parents. It demonstrated the special relationship that grew between Leo, Mina and those who came to trust them. This was the closest they could get to 'family'.

Max never forgot the genuine interest Mina retained in the lives they had built and the families they had raised. 'You should have seen her at any of those [Buchenwald Boys] meetings! Big smile on her face, surrounded by many of us, wanting to know how we are doing, about our families, happy at good news, sad at bad news … she was always proud of our achievements.'[41]

For Mina, the Buchenwald group was one example of the many friendships that were established between the 'helper' and the 'helped' in those formative post-war years of resettlement and rehabilitation. 'Forty years later', Mina recalled late in her life, 'the migrants with whom I worked still consider me their friend. I am invited to all their Simchas [life cycle events]'.[42]

Leo too would step up to help individuals, often at a moment's notice. 'He was one of the people', Mina said of her husband. 'Although he was President of the Society and very occupied with matters of policy, it was nothing for him to pick up a suitcase of a new arrival and shift this young man from Burke Rd to a room in St Kilda or Kew or any part of the world, he was just that sort of man.'[43]

A Sacred Mission

At the time, many new arrivals were unconcerned and unaware of the reasons that drove those Jews who had been spared the brunt of Hitler's brutal 'Final Solution' to rescue and help those who had not. What motivated individuals like Leo and Mina to help total strangers? Mina's deep connection with those who had experienced the horrors of the Holocaust, was in part because of the pain she too felt. Though not a 'survivor' she empathised with their profound grief, their sense of loss. 'Those who came before the war felt very close to those who had suffered in Europe. Those people who had close relatives who didn't survive, felt a special bond with the survivors.' As a result, Mina channelled all her energy into community service. It became the focus of her life. Her sacred mission. 'After the war, the shock of what had happened touched me greatly. I put all my efforts into relief fund work ...'[44] For Leo, the emotional connection with the horrors confronted by European Jewry also ran deep. 'The Holocaust shattered me', he wrote to his rabbi, shortly before he died.[45]

When Leo returned from his trip to Europe and Mandatory Palestine in 1946, he spoke of the 'sacred work of rescue and rehabilitation' of the 'ashes of the *kedoshim* [the holy ones] scattered by the winds' and of those who were 'miraculously saved from the Nazi butchers and mass graves'.[46] Although Leo and Mina were not devout orthodox Jews, Leo instinctively invoked biblical terms. Leo's experience with survivors desperate to escape Europe confirmed what he already felt and knew. This was as much a spiritual undertaking as it was a moral obligation, not only to those who had survived but to those who had not. If the death of the 6 million was to mean anything it was to ensure a Jewish future. The fate of all Jews was tied up with those survivors who needed to step out of the darkness, to re-join the world, to be able to live again. The world they all shared depended on it.

Chapter 8

'THE LUCKY FIFTIES'

On New Year's Eve 1949, the *Australian Women's Weekly*, the most popular women's magazine of the post-war years, anticipated the arrival of a new, promising decade. 'What will they be known as, these fifties? The lucky fifties would be nice to live in.' Following the carnage of two world wars and a crippling Great Depression, 'lucky' was what most Australians hoped for.[1]

But the 'lucky' decade came to mean different things to different people.

For Leo and Mina Fink the 1950s was an expansive, personally fulfilling decade. Leo maintained his commitment to and involvement in the growing family business. He was joint managing director of United Woollen Mills Pty Ltd, manufacturers of blankets, woollen and worsted materials, in South Melbourne and United Carpet Mills Pty Ltd, manufacturers of Wilton, Axminster and broadloom carpets, in Preston. Prosperity enabled both Leo and Mina to enjoy the benefits of a good life. They were active participants in Melbourne's expanding social and cultural scene. Family photos of Leo and Mina in formal dinner attire, at social gatherings, charity balls, family celebrations, or in holiday mode at the family beach house in Gould Street, Frankston, are all testament to a zest for life that they lovingly shared with many. Most importantly, good fortune empowered them to engage in their life's true passion. As leaders in social welfare, voluntary communal work remained the focus of their very public lives.

It was a decade that saw Leo and Mina travel the globe, participate in international conferences, receive recognition for their charitable work, further their communal aspirations and expand their leadership roles. From the time they left Bialystok, Leo and Mina were citizens of the world, deeply connected to global events, particularly those that impacted on the Jewish world they cherished. The 1950s was a transformative decade, not just for Leo and Mina, but for the land they had grown to love and call home. Australia was coming of age.

The Arts – A Time for Innovation, a Time for Restoration

The 1950s has been unfairly branded as a dull, boring decade. Australia, we have been led to believe, was stuck in a social and political rut, only to be jolted out of its bland complacency by the sudden arrival of the revolutionary and liberating 'swinging sixties'. Nothing could be further from the truth. The 1950s was a time in which Australians began to discover themselves and the world to which they belonged.

The arts were at the forefront of social change for many Australians. Ray Lawler's play *Summer of the Seventeenth Doll* was first performed at the Union Theatre in Melbourne, on 28 November 1955. It marked a turning point in Australian theatre by accurately depicting a distinctly Australian way of life in its own characteristic idiom, complete with working class, naturalistic characters and domestic tensions that were gritty and authentic.[2] The 1955 Australian film *Jedda* was written, produced and directed by Charles Chauvel, an innovative Australian filmmaker. His last film, it is notable for being the first to star two indigenous actors, Robert Tudawali and Ngarla Kunoth in the leading roles. It was also the first Australian feature film to be shot in colour.

The film received international acclaim and was nominated for the Golden Palm Award at the 1955 Cannes Film Festival.[3]

For Melbourne's rapidly growing Jewish immigrant community, the 1950s was a decade of restoration and recovery. The Kadimah of the 1950s in Lygon Street Carlton remained the cultural hub of communal life, a safe space that was familiar and nurturing, a place that could reclaim a lost cultural world. This 'new' community was not in search of the avant-garde or the experimental. It did not seek innovation, it was a return to the 'old' world that they longed for most, an old world that had to find its place in a strange, new world.

By 1953 Kadimah membership had grown to over 1300. Many were not post-war refugees, but pre-war immigrants like the Finks, who retained strong ties to the cultural world the Kadimah represented. Leo and Mina, though comfortable moving within both Jewish and non-Jewish circles, remained lifelong supporters of the Kadimah, both as philanthropists and patrons. For this was still a part of their world, a world they too had left behind. 'In the early years, it was the only place I really felt at home', Mina mused.

The Kadimah was home to the David Herman Theatre, a group of enthusiastic amateurs under the expert guidance of professionals Jacob Waislitz and Rachel Holzer, a drama society that regularly staged several plays a year, each with ten or more performances, playing to capacity audiences.[4] At the same time, these plays were a timely reminder of the contemporary social issues that surrounded everyday life, then and now. Little wonder that it was the well-known, popular Yiddish plays from the past that resonated most strongly, that captured their hearts and their minds. When, in 1957, Jacob Waislitz reprised his famous 1920 Warsaw production of the The Dybbuk, a tragic love story of unrequited love, of wandering souls trapped between two worlds, it struck a particularly poignant chord with its audience. Many knew the story well, but could also identify as Jewish wanderers themselves, trapped between two worlds, the old and the new. These plays were a glimpse of a life and a world once lived, but lived no more. For these Jews, Yiddish theatre was a celebration of the familiar, a means of connection with the past.[5]

The Kadimah housed an expansive library with thousands of books, overseas newspapers and journals, connecting this community with the Jewish world. A full-time librarian was employed to handle the demand. The Kadimah also hosted a vast public program, lectures, musical soirees, information evenings with local personalities and an increasing number of visiting overseas academics and theatrical impresarios. Yiddish films produced in the pre-war years, such as the 1936 musical comedy hit *Yidl mitn Fidl* (Jew with His Fiddle) were often shown to appreciative audiences hungry to see again that which had thrilled and entertained them in bygone times. Throughout the 1950s the Kadimah became a world within a world, an active, socially engaged institution that busily operated throughout the week and on weekends.

The Jewish 'newcomers' were comforted by the familiar, nurtured by a cultural world they brought with them. Here they could recreate a parallel universe 'down under', not charged by novelty but by the surety of the past. On the other hand, Australian popular culture was ready for the more radical, for the shock of the new. Audiences welcomed the likes of 'Edna Everage', a satirical character performed by Barry Humphries, who first appeared at a Christmas revue in December 1955. 'Edna', the fictional housewife from Moonee Ponds, would go on to entertain local and international audiences for decades.[6] Johnny O'Keefe released 'The Wild One' on 5 July 1958, considered by many

Leo (centre middle row) in Maccabi soccer team Bialystok 1920

Leo (left) the pioneer in Mandatory Palestine 1921

Top left: Leo (centre) with fellow
students in Berlin circa 1925

Top right: Leo the new immigrant
1928

Bottom left: Fink brothers from
left, Jack, Leo, Sid and Wolf in
Berwick 1929

Top: Leo and Mina's
engagement in Bialystok 1932

Right: Leo and Mina in
Bialystok 1932

Mina (second from left) with friends in Bialystok 1938

Mina (first on right, second row) graduates from St John Ambulance 1940

Mina circa 1940s

UJORF Medical Relief Mission 1946

This is Jewish Life in Europe Today!

UJORF Appeal

Mina (first on left) in London, International Council of Jewish Women Convention 1954

Leo (second from left) in Ashdod early 1960s

Leo and Mina in Israel early 1960s

Opening of AWI in Ashdod 1963

Arthur Calwell and Leo Fink at the *Johan de Witt* 20 year reunion

Mina elected National President NCJW
1967

Leo Fink memorial

LEO FINK

1901 — 1972

President:

United Jewish Overseas Relief Fund 1942-1947

Australian Jewish Welfare & Relief Society 1947-1960

Mina meets Leah Rabin in Jerusalem 1976

Mina with Prime Minister Bob Hawke mid 1980s

Opening ceremony of Jewish Holocaust Centre 1984; (far right) Mina in sunglasses

Mina and the Holocaust museum's volunteer survivor guides in 1985

Mina and her Buchenwald Boys celebrate 40 years of survival

National Council of Jewish Women

The COUNCIL BULLETIN

שנה טובה

Volume 64 Number 4 SEPTEMBER 1990 - 5749

NCJW LOSES A GREAT LEADER.
In Memoriam Mina Fink MBE
1914 - 1990

National Council of Jewish Women of Australia deeply grieves the passing on 2nd May 1990, of its dearly beloved and admired leader, colleague and friend.

N.C.J.W. was privileged by Mina Fink's many years of unswerving commitment, leadership and support. She was the President of N.C.J.W. Victoria from 1957-1960, N.C.J.W. National President from 1967 to 1973, N.C.J.W. Honorary Life Governor, and a Vice President and Honorary Life Member of the Executive of the International Council of Jewish Women.

Miriam Mina Fink (nee Waks) was born in Bialystok, Poland the daughter of a family with a Chassidic background. After matriculating in 1932 she married Leo Fink and emigrated to Australia. She became an active member of the Melbourne Jewish community soon after the birth of her children, Freda and Nathan. From 1943-1947 Director of the United Jewish Overseas Relief Fund and President of its Ladies Group 1945-47. She travelled extensively interstate and overseas with her late husband, founder of

UJORF, to rally support for the rescue and rehabilitation of the survivors of the Nazi holocaust.

In 1947, when the Welfare Society amalgamated with the Relief Fund, she became Director of the Australian Jewish Welfare and Relief Society, a position she held for many years. In the early fifties Mina became actively involved in the NCJW and by 1954 attended her first ICJW Convention in London. Since then she attended most ICJW Conventions, and held the position of ICJW Chairman, Resolution

and By-Laws, and Vice President.

After serving as Victorian Section President 1958-1960, she became National President of NCJW 1967-1973. Her ties with Israel date back to her early childhood and maternal Zionist grandfather - Elieser Kaplan. She visited Israel on numerous occasions. She recalled with pride the exciting event of the official opening of the Wool Tops Factory in Ashdod, 1963, a venture her late husband founded. In 1968 she accompanied her husband to the first Economic Conference convened by the Prime Minister, L. Eshkol. In 1974 she was awarded an M.B.E. by the Queen and the citation reads:

"For Community Services, particularly Jewish Women"

Mina Fink was an Executive member of the Z.F.A. for almost two decades. She was instrumental in building the Holocaust Museum in Melbourne and encouraged its volunteer and educational programs. She was Chairman of the Australian Jewish Welfare Appeal - Melbourne, 1987.

Mina Fink obituary

to be the birth of Australian rock 'n' roll. It became an international hit and would be recorded by Buddy Holly and Jerry Lee Lewis.[7]

Iconic Australian novels of the decade include Frank Hardy's *Power Without Glory* (1950), Neville Shute's *A Town Like Alice* (1950), Alan Marshall's *I Can Jump Puddles* (1955), D'Arcy Niland's *The Shiralee* (1955). All were subsequently made into films, but none more famously than Neville Shute's *On the Beach* (1957), a grim post-apocalyptic drama that depicted the aftermath of nuclear war. The film, produced and directed by Stanley Kramer, brought Hollywood to Melbourne when filming took place in early 1959. Never before had Melbourne hosted the likes of Gregory Peck, Ava Gardner, Fred Astaire and Anthony Perkins.[8] The first Miles Franklin Literary Award was given in 1957 to Patrick White for his fifth novel *Voss*, based on the life of explorer Ludwig Leichhardt.[9]

The controversial Jewish writer Judah Waten, born in Odessa to Russian immigrants, published his most celebrated and critically acclaimed novel, *Alien Son*, in 1952, describing his own experiences as a young Jewish boy growing up in Perth and Melbourne after the First World War. *Alien Son* was arguably the first Australian novel to deal with the migrant experiences of a non–Anglo Saxon. Waten wrote in English but was also a notable translator of Yiddish texts.[10]

With increased demand, Yiddish literature gained in popularity. More than 40 Yiddish books were published in Melbourne after 1950.[11] Mendl Balberyszki's Jewish bookstore at 108 Rathdowne Street in Carlton became something of an institution. Throughout the 1950s the community was able to support two Jewish newspapers, each with a Yiddish supplement. Leo and Mina were well known as financial patrons of a number of Yiddish writers, in particular the prize-winning

Herz Bergner and fellow Bialystoker, the writer, editor and translator, Yehoshua Rapaport.[12]

Prosperity and Opportunity

A bold immigration program brought a diverse multicultural population to these shores long before the word 'multicultural' became common currency. By 1954, 17,300 Jewish immigrants were part of this evolving 'new' Australia, more than doubling the size of the Jewish population. Of those, 10,380 (over 60 per cent) settled in Victoria, most in Melbourne. At the same time, Carlton, the first home of the Finks and other Eastern European Jews, began a slow downward trend as a place of Jewish settlement, one that continued into the 1960s. Some, like Leo and Mina had moved east to the more affluent suburb of Kew more than a decade earlier, others began the shift to Balwyn or increasingly to the southern suburbs of Caulfield, St Kilda or Elwood. The northern suburbs like Northcote, Preston and Brunswick saw new communities expand as places of first settlement in the immediate post-war years.[13]

High immigration and economic prosperity went hand in hand. The post-war years were economic boom times for business. From 1947 to 1972 Australia enjoyed a buoyant economy. Only two brief periods, cyclic downturns in 1952 and 1961, interrupted this prosperity. It was a good time for manufacturing. Like the Finks, many Jews from Eastern Europe brought their 'old world' occupations with them; knitters, weavers, shoemakers, tailors, leather merchants and manufacturers set up shop and prospered.[14]

Global politics was never far away. Jews were acutely aware of how quickly things could change, even in a 'lucky' country as far away as Australia. With the emergence of the Soviet Union as a post-war superpower, Australia was caught up in the politics of the Cold War. A fear of 'reds under the beds' and subversive fifth columns terrified the nation, also fuelled by the notorious Petrov spy affair of 1954. The Korean civil war 1950 to 1953 saw Australia commit 17,000 troops to fight alongside the US and South Korean soldiers. Australia sustained 1500 casualties and 339 deaths. When the Soviets launched *Sputnik 1* the first artificial satellite to orbit the earth, on 4 October 1957, there were fears that they could also launch ballistic missiles armed with nuclear weapons.

But the scourge of antisemitism, the greatest destroyer of Jewish life, was still only a benign presence in Australia, one that lurked in some social circles but remained largely populist and never posed an existential threat. Leo and Mina firmly believed that any future threat to Jewish life could be countered by a strong, resilient community, one that remained connected to Jewish humanity and the greater Jewish world, a world that now included Israel. Such a community could and would prevail.

The rise of consumerism and the abundance of new gadgets and homeware innovations were hallmarks of this 'lucky', prosperous decade. They were designed to enhance the home and family, still perceived, in the 1950s, as the cornerstone of a stable and moral society.[15] Home and family were also central to traditional Jewish values, the wellspring of Jewish life, taking on even greater significance following the devastation of the Holocaust, an event that continued to cast its shadow over the community.

Holocaust commemorations grew in importance and significance throughout the 1950s. By 1957 over 3000 attended the anniversary of the Warsaw ghetto uprising, the precursor of future Holocaust commemorations, at the Melbourne Town Hall. Many hundreds more were turned away because the hall was at capacity.[16] Over the years, the impact and devastation of the Holocaust remained a key motivator for the type of lives Leo and Mina chose to lead and the decisions they made. In the last decade of her life, Mina's engagement with the Holocaust would take on a new direction, one that went far beyond memorialisation. It would be her last enduring legacy.

In the 1950s Australia was rapidly becoming a land of opportunity, a land where middle-class aspirations and hard work were rewarded. Prime minister Robert Menzies' vision of a new Australia was built on the back of an independent, self-reliant middle class, Menzies' 'forgotten people' who rejected inherited wealth as the precursor to success. These were, in Menzies' own words, 'the strivers, the planners, the ambitious ones', the 'salary earners, shop keepers, skilled artisans, professional men and women'. It was a muscular and robust vision, in which 'leaners grow flabby, lifters grow muscle'. This was the new Australia in which initiative was prized, 'for men without ambition become slaves'. This was the land where private aspiration met public benefit.[17] Middle-class aspirations, self-reliance and independence were traits also entrenched in Jewish cultural life. Leo and Mina fitted right in.

The Early Fifties for the Finks and the AJWRS

In 1950 Leo was president of the Australian Jewish Welfare and Relief Society (AJWRS) and vice president of the Federation of Australian Jewish Welfare Societies. Mina was a director and an executive member of the AJWRS. Under their leadership the AJWRS continued to expand and develop its mandate and outreach, pivoting quickly to meet new social challenges that confronted the community while taking advantage of any emerging opportunities.

On 1 March 1950, Leo, Mina and their 17-year-old daughter, Freda, left for a nine-month tour of Europe and Israel. They travelled on the SS *Himalaya* arriving in London on 30 March. Not content to be idle tourists they spent their time as guests of HIAS and the Joint, visiting refugee camps, health institutions, children's homes and Jewish educational and vocational institutions. They returned home with a new-found understanding of the formidable challenges that still lay ahead for the Jewish world and what would be required to meet those challenges.[18]

At the AJWRS annual general meeting on 27 November 1950 Leo and Mina tallied the highest number of votes in board elections, in spite of their absence for most of the year. The minutes of the AGM laid out some of those challenges, most of which still concerned new arrivals.

> During the past year 3000 Jewish immigrants arrived in Australia (1949 = 3800). Out of those nearly 2000 settled in Victoria ... All this requires large funds ... at the Frances Barkman House (formerly Larino Home) about 30 children are maintained requiring food, clothing, education, etc ... The monies received from overseas were for capital use only, and with this money hostels were purchased ... The AJWRS had at the time of the meeting seven houses. More were needed ... At the end of October, there were in Europe 3800 permit holders, nearly all will need to be helped with transport costs and housing.[19]

Shortly after, on 30 January 1951 Mina was elected to four welfare committees: Education, Accommodation, Sustenance and Reception, all of which dealt with domestic matters. Her passion for the welfare of children remained a primary function of the relief work she undertook throughout the first half of this decade. Mina advised the AJWRS Board on 10 April 1951 that she had made the decision that goods sent to Oeuvre de Secours aux Enfants (Children's Aid Society) France had been redirected to Israel, as the need there was greater. At the same time, she reported that the Frances Barkman House (FBH) was accommodating 27 children, but stressed the need for additional housing for younger children to support parents in temporary hardship. To impress the urgency of the matter she insisted that a visit to FBH be organised for AJWRS Board members to inspect the premises.[20]

By mid-June of that year, Mina urged the AJWRS to establish a creche at FBH so that children could be left there during the day, enabling both parents to work. She felt 'happy to see arrangements enabling the admission of younger children of the age group two to five'. In August, Mina was concerned with the number of sick children at FBH whom she felt 'would benefit from a trained social worker'. The increasing involvement of trained social workers was welcomed and understood by Mina who was always a stickler for the professionalisation of services and procedures whenever appropriate. As the decade progressed the role of volunteers shifted away from direct care responsibility and more to administrative matters. Mina embraced change that she viewed as beneficial. She was always one who could read and move with the current of the times. By November of that year Mina joined a Special Committee to investigate the urgent need for a home for small children that would be staffed by fully trained professionals.[21]

At the same time Leo remained engaged with international matters, this time he turned his focus to the treatment of Hungarian Jews and lodged a protest with the United Nations through Canberra. In August 1951 Leo had a personal meeting with Tasman Heyes, secretary of the Department of Immigration. Heyes subsequently 'promised to speed up all application for permits concerning nominees in Hungary, and also Hungarian nominees in other European countries'.[22] Leo always valued face-to-face meetings when seeking resolutions to pressing concerns. He never hesitated to travel in order to make his point in person. By the end of 1951, with nearly 4000 permit holders still in Europe awaiting transportation to Australia, accommodating new arrivals still remained the main concern for the AJWRS. Employment for unskilled workers proved more difficult, temporarily impacted by the downturn in the economy. The need for more accommodation for young children was also stressed. FBH was stretched to the limit, with alterations and reorganisation urgently needed.

On 11 December 1951 Leo was unanimously re-elected president of the AJWRS. Mina was elected deputy delegate to the Victorian Jewish Board of Deputies (VJBD) and re-elected president of the Ladies' Group.

By the end of 1952 Leo noted that 'the centre of gravity has shifted from immigration to rehabilitation'. In a letter to Lewis Neikrug at HIAS Paris on 2 December 1952 Leo reiterated his understanding that all immigrants had to become self-sufficient: 'Our task has become one of consolidation and absorption with the view of making every new settler a self-supporting and happy citizen'.[23] Leo and Mina fully understood that successful integration into the community was weighted by each newcomer becoming a 'lifter and not a leaner'.

The task of absorption and integration remained the focus of 1953 welfare work. 'Activities of the society', wrote Leo, 'have shifted from mass immigration to rehabilitation and integration of newcomers to this country … The necessity for assisting needy Jewish residents in Melbourne became more acute, and the Society did its best to help everyone who came for help' This was only possible, Leo emphasised 'through the financial assistance of the American Joint Distribution Committee'.[24]

International Recognition for Leo

In the 1950s Leo's prodigious efforts in immigration and welfare were being recognised both within the Commonwealth and by international Jewry. In 1953 Leo received his first significant international award, the Coronation Medal from Buckingham Palace, in honour of the Queen's coronation on 2 June 1953. Governments of various countries in the British Commonwealth determined the list of recipients. While neither Leo nor Mina actively sought recognition, the award was public acknowledgement from those outside the Jewish world of the nature and scope of relief work Leo personally shouldered.

In 1959 at the close of the decade Leo received the United HIAS Service Award of Honour, with this citation:

> In recognition of his significant contributions to the field of Jewish migration and resettlement and to the general community welfare. His spirit of humanitarian concern for his fellow man prompted his colleagues who have worked by his side to adjudge him to be the leader in his community worthy of this Award which carried with it the profound gratitude of United HIAS Service, and the countless human beings the agency has rescued and helped to find security and opportunity in countries of haven.[25]

These type of awards pleased Mina, not out of self-congratulation or vanity, but because she held firm that public recognition for personal effort was a worthy aspiration.

International Connections, New Directions

Leo and Mina embarked on another overseas trip in 1954. Again, their visit to London and New York facilitated numerous meetings with Jewish organisations, strengthening international connections that both

Leo and Mina saw as essential for a robust, resilient Jewish world. This time Mina, who had joined the National Council of Jewish Women in 1946, attended the International Council of Jewish Women conference in London, an indication that Mina was now primed to set her own course. It was her first experience as a conference attendee on the international stage in her own right. It would not be her last.

Leo's authority and public standing on migration matters saw him chair the Migration Standing Committee for the Executive Council of Australian Jewry (ECAJ) for a ten-year period, from 1950 to 1960. In 1954 and 1955 he also served as vice president of the Victorian Jewish Board of Deputies.

By the end of 1955 Leo shared his global vision for the AJWRS to associate with the Jewish World Migration Council in New York, establishing an International Committee which would enable large-scale future immigration. Leo always kept an eye on the big picture. For Leo, strength lay not only in numbers but in unity. Great achievement lay in the ability for international organisations to work together. This would also become Mina's strength in the years that lay ahead.

1956 – A Landmark Year

For Australia, 1956 was a big year. The Olympic Games came to Melbourne and television became a central feature of Australian living rooms. It was also the year that the British began their atomic tests at Maralinga, Hungarian refugees arrived after their failed uprising against suffocating Soviet dictatorship, the Suez Canal crisis saw our prime minister Robert Menzies strut the international stage in a bid to halt the impasse. In June 1956 the first polio vaccine was rolled out to the nation.[26]

For Leo and Mina Fink, 1956 was an expansive year that was still dominated by matters of welfare and communal affairs. In addition to his many public roles, Leo was both acting president and acting treasurer of the ECAJ. The Australian Jewish Welfare and Relief Society's annual report was testament to the vast scope and outreach of its various operations. But changes were afoot.

'The days of mass migration have ended', Leo's 1956 AJWRS AGM report boldly announced. 'In the past 12 months about 1000 Jews were admitted to this country'. However, the uprising in Hungary and the revolution in Egypt saw the AJWRS come to the rescue of additional Jewish refugees seeking asylum. Leo foresaw the possibility of a next wave of Polish Jews who were still residing in communist Poland also requiring assistance from the AJWRS for immigration and resettlement. However, 'assistance and rehabilitation of Jewish victims of Nazi persecution is still our main function … The office received nearly 5000 letters and sent out 8500 communications and more than 8000 persons came to us during the past 12 months'.[27]

Welfare work increasingly focused on the incapacitated, those requiring sustenance payments, support for temporary sick leave, medical care, post hospitalisation care, and support for students. Additionally, there was an increasing number of the elderly who were ineligible for the pension. These were mostly Holocaust survivors who had not been resident in Australia for the past 20 years. The main aged care facility, the Montefiore Home was at capacity. The arrival of a number of elderly Hungarian immigrants placed another burden on limited resources.

Adequate accommodation was still a concern. Hostels remained fully occupied. Assistance came from the Bialystoker Centre and the Radomer Centre, both of which temporarily housed 119 persons including 46 children. Renovations and extensions were carried out, particularly in the Camberwell hostel.

The AJWRS Search Bureau contended with 400 inquiries from overseas for friends and relatives in Australia. While Mina was not personally responsible for these processes, she was adamant that accurate record keeping and office procedures remain professional and up to date. As a result, over 95 per cent of these individuals were able to be located through internal records, files and registers.

The Frances Barkman House remained the only Jewish children's home. It was home to 32 children in 1956, most were either orphans, children from broken homes, working widows and invalids. The operations of the home became increasingly professionalised, with administrative oversight handled by a board of management of which Mina was an active member.

AJWRS – the Heart of Communal Life

By the end of 1956 the AJWRS was the beating heart of a vast communal, organisational network with a paid membership of well over 500 individuals. The AJWRS had one paid secretary and an accountant. Its offices at 443 Little Collins Street were a central hub of community activities, available to a range of organisations: the Melbourne Jewish Philanthropic Society, the Melbourne Jewish Aid Society, the Jewish Orphan and Children's Aid Society, the United Restitution Organisation and the Jewish Mutual Loan Company. 'All these Societies make common use of the excellent facilities, central location, trained office staff', Leo reported. The board room was used by the ECAJ, B'nai B'rith, National Council of Jewish Women, the Melbourne Hebrew Ladies' Benevolent Society, a number of *Landsmanshaftn* and a number of smaller charitable organisations.[28]

The AJWRS operated under an executive of seven officers and ten board members, all volunteers. Six committees oversaw the main functions of the organisation; Immigration, Frances Barkman House, Sustenance, Employment, Accommodation and Membership. Each committee was chaired by a dedicated, hardworking volunteer. The overwhelming majority of the executive and board were Eastern European pre-war and post-war Jewish immigrants, many with differing points of view and political affiliations but all operated within a democratic framework. Arguments were had over principles and practices but in general they addressed core concerns. What was best for the Jewish community? How could they underpin and ensure Jewish continuity? Opinions may have varied but they all had one thing in common. They shared Leo and Mina's vision for strengthening and fortifying Melbourne's Jewish community, ensuring the welfare of its constituents while remaining in solidarity with and connected to world Jewry. Leo and Mina had built an organisation in their own image.

A New Direction for Mina

By the middle of June 1957 Mina had increased her involvement with the National Council of Jewish Women (NCJW). It also pointed to Mina's calculated move away from a hands-on role with the AJWRS while still remaining an influential member of its decision-making board. Clearly it was time for Mina to forge ahead. There were new heights to scale.

The NCJW was a broad-based organisation founded in 1923 in Sydney by Dr Fanny Reading, a young Sydney doctor who had been born in Minsk in 1884, before migrating to Australia with her family in 1890. Her mandate for the NCJW was founded on four pillars:

'Religion, Education, Philanthropy, Social'. The Sydney-based organisation quickly became a national movement. In 1948, on the NCJW's 25th anniversary, Dr Reading pointed to her reasons for establishing such a women's organisation, 'I felt the need of organised Jewish Womanhood in Australia, who would play their part, and take their place in the life of the community and in the life of the bigger community, the world ...' Dr Reading was also a strong advocate for a Jewish State and a lifelong supporter of Israel. She was adamant that the NCJW also adopt local non-Jewish causes as part of its charitable outreach, thereby demonstrating that Jewish women had an important role to play in the wider community. For Dr Reading, it was all about building a national sisterhood where women could reach their full potential, as individuals and as Jews.[29]

For Mina this was an organisation that spoke to all her sensibilities, from her earliest days in Bialystok at the progressive, liberal, co-educational Druskin Gymnasium where intellectual pursuits were not hindered by her gender, to her lifelong commitment to social action and the welfare of those less fortunate. Here, she could hone her interest in the work of women in voluntary communal organisations both at a local and international level and the need to empower them to do more, to strive to reach beyond their grasp.

Initially Mina's focus still remained with assisting new immigrants. That month's NCJW Bulletin reported that 'Mrs L Fink, Convenor of the [Welfare] Section and her co-workers are doing a grand job in coping with the needs of a steady stream of Hungarian refugees and their families'. Two things to note were her continued empathy with those in urgent need of assistance and her ability to enlist support from co-workers and be a team builder, traits that first came to the fore during her work in the war years.[30]

Mina's involvement advanced swiftly. In the August – September 1957 NCJW Bulletin a major announcement was made. Mina Fink was the newly elected Victorian president, a delegate to the United Nations Organisation and convenor of the Welfare Group. Mina's decision to stand for office was whole heartedly supported by Leo. While Mina never operated in Leo's shadow, always following her own pathway, showing initiative and independent decision making, this was a major step up as a leader in her own right, in her own organisation. It was a powerful indication of Mina's personal growth and development.[31]

In February 1958 Mina attended the NCJW conference in Sydney where she presented an overview of the Victorian Branch activities. 'Growth and expansion in membership and projects; for the first time, projects are being specifically promoted in the name of the NCJW in Israel; local welfare work continues with Hungarian refugees; local work with non-Jewish organisations includes Meals on Wheels.' Mina's vision and capacity for hard work were contributing to the NCJW's core mission.

In Mina's first annual report for the NCJW in May 1958, she declared 'United we stand – Divided we fall'. It was a mantra that emphasised teamwork, a feature of her leadership style. In the same month, Mina 'was honoured by invitation to attend a Women's Morning Tea tendered by all Women's organisations to the Queen Mother during her Melbourne visit'. For Mina, this type of recognition acknowledged her effort and achievement. It was also the type of social engagement she personally relished.[32]

At the August – September 1958 NCJW annual general meeting, Mina was re-elected Victorian president. By this time, she had engaged new interests and a younger generation, forming three new groups: the Romanian Group, the Council Younger Set and the Freelancers Group. Mina never stepped away from helping the disadvantaged.[33]

On 1 October 1958 a meeting was arranged between the AJWRS, NCJW and B'nai B'rith to establish a sheltered workshop in Melbourne for disabled young adults. This involved Mina as president of NCJW, Leo as president of AJWRS and Kurt Lippmann as B'nai B'rith representative. The sheltered workshop was opened in December 1958 in two rooms in the AJWRS building on Punt Road in South Yarra.[34]

The End of a Decade, the End of an Era

On 17 February 1958 the AJWRS confirmed the arrival of a rising number of new immigrants. Although these numbers did not rival those of the early post-war period, they nevertheless contributed to ongoing concerns over absorption and integration. 'The Jewish community of Australia has risen by seven per cent during the past year, owing to the immigration of several thousand refugees from Hungary, Egypt and Poland ... 1958 would bring a further influx of migrants mainly from Eastern European countries.'[35]

In the following year Leo reported on the continuing expansive outreach of the welfare organisation.

> The total Jewish migrants for Australia was 1466 of which Victoria received 868 ... the majority of migrants to Victoria came from Poland, and of the 580 Polish migrants who arrived in Australia, 450 settled in Victoria. Although the Welfare Society was not instrumental in obtaining permits or arranging transportation for Israeli migrants, it was frequently called upon for assistance in the various fields of social services ... About 12,000 people have called upon us in matters of migration, transportation, loans, sustenance, as well as for general advice. Outgoing correspondence exceeded 10,000 mail pieces, not including 11,000 circular letters which were distributed during the year and incoming letters from overseas and within Australia were over 7000.[36]

Throughout 1959 Leo became increasingly cognisant that the days of mass immigration and resettlement were coming to an end, that Jewish Welfare would have to be reset to undertake new challenges, particularly those surrounding a fast-approaching ageing population. The tide was turning. Leo was also ready to move on, to hand over the reins. He would do so in 1960, to the energetic and indefatigable Hamburg born pre-war immigrant Walter Lippmann, a man of vision, a man that Leo knew was a builder and innovator.

Towards the end of the 'lucky' decade, and in spite of their considerable commitments and responsibilities, Leo and Mina continued to travel. In 1958 they went to Japan, visiting Nara and Tokyo. Japan was not a destination frequented by many Australian tourists in that first decade after the war. The scars and wounds of a bloody conflict ran deep. Memories were still raw. But Leo and Mina remained excited, curious and interested in the world around them.

In the latter half of 1959 Leo and Mina travelled to Sweden where Leo was a delegate representing Australian Jewry at the World Jewish Congress Assembly in Stockholm. On their return they stopped over in Israel, a place that was not only close to their hearts but a place that was becoming increasingly important in the Jewish world. Again, with an eye to the future, Leo began to explore a bold new idea that would test his resolve like never before. But Leo the visionary now had a life partner who not only shared his world view, his dreams and aspirations but who also encouraged him to pursue them. This new venture would underscore their commitment to strengthening a resilient Jewish world with Israel at its core.

Leo, the Zionist pioneer, was about to return to the place where it all began. Full circle.

Chapter 9

A PIONEER ONCE MORE

Leo Fink never forgot his time as a young pioneer in Mandatory Palestine. Leo, the idealist, never forgot what it felt like to be part of something greater than himself, of building a new future in a new land, of chasing a dream. 'I am a romantic at heart', he once recalled, attributing his creative energy to a 'type of restlessness'. It came as no surprise when he jumped at the opportunity to be a pioneer once more.[1]

In late 1959, while visiting Israel, Leo was approached by the Israeli minister of commerce and industry, Pinchas Sapir, to explore the possibility of starting up a business venture in Israel. The thought of bolstering Israel's economy, of contributing to its economic growth and empowering the small nation to become more financially independent and resilient, appealed to Leo and Mina's sensibilities. It sat well within their world view. Passionate Zionists, they believed that a strong, robust Israel was a way of strengthening and ensuring the continuity of the Jewish world. For Leo, this was never going to be about personal gain or profit. 'The principle', Leo said, 'was more important than dividends'. Bigger issues were at play.[2]

It signalled the end of one chapter of their lives and the start of another. The year 1960 saw Mina Fink in her last year as president of the National Council of Jewish Women, Victoria Section. Leo Fink relinquished his presidency of the Australian Jewish Welfare and Relief Society.

Friends and Enemies

By 1960, the fledgling Jewish state had fought two wars since declaring independence in 1948 and remained surrounded by hostile enemies, hell bent on its destruction and vowing to 'push the Jews into the sea'. Israel could not afford to let its guard down. Consequently, Israel had to retain a powerful, vigilant and extremely costly military. Compulsory military service for both men and women was a feature of Israeli life. Khaki uniformed young soldiers were a common sight on the dusty streets of Tel Aviv, the ancient alleyways of Jerusalem and the port city of Haifa. If recent history had taught Jews like Leo and Mina anything, it was that Jews had to be self-reliant and resourceful. You had to back yourself. The young nation knew that it had to fight its own battles. Jewish survival depended on it.

Militarily, Israel was strong, but the nation's leaders knew that its survival also depended on winning the all-important diplomatic war, a war that was highly politicised and factionalised. Israel needed to garner more international support. Its enemies were numerous, its friends few. In the 1950s and '60s the belligerent Arab nations were strongly backed by the Soviet Union, by now a forceful superpower, and members of its expansive Soviet bloc: Bulgaria, Cuba, East Germany, Czechoslovakia, Poland, Hungary and Romania. At the same time the United Kingdom, United States of America and France supported the notion of 'non-aggression' between Israel and the Arab nations and retained a cool, but strategic 'friendship'. The Scandinavian countries of Sweden, the Netherlands, Denmark and Norway all voted for partition and fostered good relations with Israel throughout the 1950s and '60s but their influence on the international arena was limited. India, not wanting to antagonise its large Muslim population, voted against partition but allowed a consulate to open in Mumbai in 1953.

The Indian–Israeli relationship remained frigid until the early 1990s. China abstained from voting in the UN Partition Plan, expressed support for the Palestinian right of return but refrained from denying Israel's right to exist. Relations with China remained distant until the 1980s. Iran developed good relationships with Israel after it came under the rule of the Shah in 1953 but soured and dissolved after the Iranian revolution of 1978.[3]

From the mid-1950s to the late 1960s, Israel's foreign affairs policies enjoyed considerable success amongst many new emerging nations in Africa. Financial, agricultural and scientific aid led to important relationships with Liberia, Ghana, Sierra Leone, Ivory Coast, Nigeria and Uganda. In 1962, *Newsweek* called the Israeli foreign affairs program in Africa as 'one of the strangest unofficial alliances in the world'. These ties all began to unravel after the Six Day War in June 1967, a time that saw the political emergence of Yasser Arafat and growing support for his Palestinian Liberation Organization with its demands to 'liberate Palestine'. Following the Yom Kippur War and Arab oil embargo of 1973 most of the sub-Saharan countries severed diplomatic ties with Israel.[4]

Australia had a strong historical connection with Israel. Ties between the two countries were good. During the First World War, four Australian Light Horse brigades took part in the British conquest of Palestine from the Ottoman Turks in 1916–17.[5] The famous battle of Beersheba on 31 October 1917 sealed the Aussies reputation as a nation of courageous daredevils and risk takers. The celebrated Australian military hero and leader Sir John Monash demonstrated his support for a Jewish homeland by agreeing to be the inaugural president of the Zionist Federation of Australia in 1927.[6] Although largely ceremonial, his position was a powerful statement from a man Australians revered and looked up to. Australian troops fought in the Middle East during the Second World War with many stationed in Mandatory Palestine where they garnered a reputation for fairness, an easy-going manner and for being sympathetic to the Jewish cause. Australia played a crucial part in the establishment of the State of Israel when Australia's foreign minister HV (Doc) Evatt served as chairman of the UN General Assembly's committee on Palestine and helped to push through the UN Partition Plan on 29 November, 1947.[7] Despite heavy pressure from the United Kingdom on its fellow Commonwealth nations to abstain on the resolution, Australia voted in favour of partition. Prime minister Ben Chifley formally recognised Israel on 28 January 1949, making Australia one of the first countries to do so.[8]

Leo foresaw that what was a firm political relationship could be extended and enhanced. An Australian business venture in Israel, the first of its kind, would build on already solid foundations between the two countries, but this time it would be based on a mutually beneficial, yet largely unexplored, economic relationship. It would be a game changer. Politics aside, it made good business sense. And Leo knew all about good business and how to build networks.

Israel – A Land of Immigrants

In 1960, Israel's population was only 2,114,000. Of that, 88.9 per cent were Jews, 7.7 per cent were Muslims, 2.3 per cent were Christians and 1.1 per cent were Druze, a close knit, unique religious and ethnic group, whose traditions incorporate elements of Islam, Hinduism and even classical Greek philosophy. While Jews made up the overwhelming majority, the country had a diverse population drawn from disparate corners of the globe. Only 37.4 per cent were native-born Israelis or 'sabras', named after the prickly pear or cactus with its thorny, tough exterior and soft centre. It was a term that came into use in the early 1930s to describe the characteristics of the 'new' resilient Jew, born of the Zionist movement in a Jewish homeland, differentiating them from the 'old' powerless Jews of the pre-war European ghettos. The rest of the population consisted of 35 per cent who were born in Europe/America and 27.6 per cent who were born in Africa/Asia.[9]

By 1960 Israel was overwhelmingly a nation of immigrants. Many were Holocaust survivors, desperate to leave the devastation of Europe behind, a continent they believed was devoid of a Jewish future. Not all who came were passionate Zionists, committed to its political ideals. Rather, they came because Israel offered them sanctuary at a time when few others did. Israel became home to many Sephardi Jews fleeing persecution in the Arab world, notably from Yemen in 1949–50 as part of Operation Magic Carpet, from Iraq in 1950–52 in Operation Ezra and Nehemiah and from Egypt after the Suez conflict in 1956 and the expulsion of foreign nationals by Egyptian president Nasser.[10] Though they all came from different backgrounds, different countries, all were united by the hope of a new life in a new homeland. From 1948 to 1961, more than a million immigrants arrived in the small, newly constituted nation, straining the resources of the Israeli Government and the Jewish Agency. Times were tough. Leo did his bit to help. He bought two properties, one in 1946 and another in 1948. All derived income remained in Israel and was given to assist his immigrant relatives living there.[11]

Israel's Economic Struggles

In the early years of nationhood, Israel's struggling economy was underpinned by large amounts of capital obtained through gifts from world Jewry. In 1948 charitable gifted contributions accounted for 33 per cent of Israel's revenue. By 1960 these contributions barely covered 8 per cent of budgetary income. Grants-in-aid from the US Government were also received in those early years, as were small amounts of capital brought in by immigrants. But the most significant boost to Israeli revenue came from reparations from the Federal Republic of Germany. The agreement, signed in September 1952 between West Germany and Israel was for three billion Deutschmarks over the next 14 years, money that was largely invested in building the country's infrastructure. The agreement was highly controversial. Public debate raged over receiving reparations from Germany, the former Nazi regime. People from both ends of the political spectrum called it 'blood money'. The most vehement opponent was the champion of the right-wing Herut party (later Likud), Menachem Begin, whose impassioned speech in the Knesset on 7 January 1952 described the act of taking money from the murderers of 6 million Jews as an act of bastardry, the greatest betrayal of the Jewish people by the Israeli Government. But prime minister David Ben Gurion and his Mapai party took a pragmatic stance, arguing that reparations were based on the recovery of as much Jewish property as possible, 'so that the murderers do not become the heirs as well'. But Begin was not swayed. 'So, you go directly to the murderers to supposedly receive the value of the homes in which your parents were burned to death. In what civilized tribe can you witness such a disgusting act?' he cried.[12] But even these highly contested and controversial payments came to an end by the early 1960s. Israel supplemented all these forms of revenue with loans, commercial credits and increasingly on foreign investment. This is where Leo stepped in.

The Push Towards Foreign Investment and Industrialisation

Leo Fink was not the only industrialist being courted by the Israeli Government to invest in Israel's future. Overtures were made to a number of prospective investors across the globe. In 1960 Pinchas Sapir invited Romanian-born Israel Pollak, a textile manufacturer who immigrated to Chile after the Second World War, to make *aliyah* (the term means to 'step up' when one goes to live in Israel) and establish a textile plant in Kiryat Gat. Pollak's new company, Polgat, grew into the largest textile, clothing and knitwear company in Israel. Eventually, Polgat became a public corporation whose shares were traded on the Tel Aviv Stock Exchange. In 1990 Israel Pollak was awarded the Israel Prize for his special contribution to society and the State of Israel. Polgat was a company that would come to have significant bearing on Leo's own enterprise in the future.

The eminent American philanthropist and textile industrialist, Israel Rogosin, was invited by Pinchas Sapir to build a rayon yarn plant in the newly established industrial city of Ashdod. Born in Belarus, Rogosin immigrated with his family to the USA in 1896, at the age of nine. He quickly showed his flair for manufacturing when his father instructed him to take over the family mill in Brooklyn at the age of 16. By 1920 he was running five mills and employing 1000 workers. Rogosin was an astute businessman and entrepreneur whose investment in the city of Ashdod in 1958 led to its rapid development. Rogosin's factory was granted 1000 dunams of land (one dunam equals 1000 square metres) for its establishment. The rayon plant opened on 9 August 1960. Rogosin continued to support the city and in February 1968 dedicated three new schools in Ashdod through contributions to the Israel Education Fund of the United States. The city of Ashdod would also become home to the first Australian enterprise to operate in Israel, with Leo at the helm.

The development of a textile and manufacturing industry throughout the 1960s became one of the largest industrial branches in Israel, second only to the foodstuff industry. In 1965 there were 1007 textile factories employing 26,300 workers, including 100 plants employing more than 50 workers each. By the late 1960s textiles constituted about 12 per cent of industrial exports. Only 4 per cent of Israelis were kibbutzniks, those living on agricultural establishments at this time. Throughout this period the kibbutzim were also undergoing a great wave of industrialisation, moving away from their farming origins towards manufacturing.[13]

Leo's Sees a Business Opportunity

Leo was fired up by the possibility of contributing to Israel's overall growth and expansion. 'The future of Israel lies in industrialization', he reported on his return from Israel in November 1959. His preliminary investigations saw a gap in the textile market.[14] The plan was to build from scratch, then manage and operate an Australian wool tops enterprise in Israel. Wool tops are the finest part of the clipped wool, and the processed tops provide the raw material for local spinners of worsted cloth. At the time, Israel was importing all its wool tops. Leo envisaged buying the raw greasy wool in Australia, then shipping it to Israel where it would be processed in an Australian-owned and managed plant. The enterprise would employ local people from the construction of the factory to its ongoing operations. The outcome would provide a competitive alternative to costly imports. The plan seemed simple. The devil lay in the detail.

Bringing Australia on Board

Leo moved swiftly to shore up support in Melbourne. While Leo would take the lead, this was something that required a team effort. Again, Leo needed an organisational structure to underpin the project and move it forward from the Australian side. More importantly, Leo needed investors.

In February 1960, Leo enlisted fellow Zionist, the prominent lawyer and then president of the Victorian Jewish Board of Deputies, Nathan Jacobson, to commence the formal requirements necessary to bring together a group of investors: a 'Board of Directors of a Syndicate'. Jacobson was born in Kiev in 1916, grew up in Warsaw and migrated to Australia in 1936. He was, like Leo, part of a group of pre-war Eastern European Jewish immigrants who became prominent community leaders, were visionaries and trailblazers.

It did not take Jacobson long to bring together a group of potential investors. On 19 February 1960 Jacobson wrote to Mr Sharef, the commercial attache, Legation of Israel, in Woollahra in NSW, advising him that a meeting had taken place in Melbourne and A£250,000 was immediately underwritten towards the cost of establishing a wool-top-making plant in Israel. They estimated that A£1,250,000 would be required to establish the plant and conduct the operation. The group proposed that an incorporated public company in Israel be established with nominal capital of A£1,000,000. Leo Fink was asked to act as chairman of the proposed company and to take charge of the plant's establishment and the conduct of the company's business. Jacobson then listed the initial requirements that Israel would need to provide in order for the operation to proceed without delay. The list was long. It focused on a number of incentives, trade concessions, subsidies and government loans. These also included the legal company

139

requirements to be set up, a long-term lease of land, the training of operators, prohibition of any other wool top plants to operate in Israel for a term of 15 years, freedom from duty and excise on machinery, raw materials, chemicals and other aids to manufacture, a subsidy for a one-year term, tax liability terms for 15 years, an arrangement for the transfer of profits and the transfer of approved investment. In response, the Israeli Ministry of Commerce and Industry insisted on face-to-face meetings.[15]

In early June 1960, Leo was given a formal farewell by the Executive Council of Australian Jewry (ECAJ), Zionist Federation of Australia, Victorian Jewish Board of Deputies, State Zionist Council of Victoria and the AJWRS. The *Australian Jewish News* boasted that 'the reception rooms of the Welfare House in Punt Road were filled to overflowing when a reception to farewell Mr Leo Fink and Mr Nathan Jacobson was held'.[16]

Leo Fink and Nathan Jacobson travelled together to lay the ground-work for the enterprise, all of which had considerable community support. Nathan Jacobson planned to stay for six weeks. Leo and Mina would spend most of the next three years in Israel. They were there throughout the entire period in which Israel made world headlines again, but not for the reasons anyone would have imagined. It had nothing to do with business. It plunged Israel, its citizens and the world right back into the heart of Holocaust darkness.

Israel Stuns the World

While doing business in Israel, with its cumbersome, officious bureau-cracy, would test Leo like never before, in other matters Israel proved itself to be most agile. Just two weeks prior to their arrival, Israel's prime minister made the most striking and bold public announcement, one that inspired Jews like Leo and Mina by its sheer audacity and daring. It also stunned the rest of the world.

On 23 May 1960 at 4pm, the prime minister of Israel, David Ben Gurion, told the Knesset, the Israeli parliament, that 'Israeli Security Services captured one of the greatest Nazi criminals Adolf Eichmann … Eichmann is already in detention in Israel and will soon be put on trial'. Former SS officer Adolf Eichmann, the infamous 'desk murderer' of the Third Reich was captured by Israeli Mossad agents in a clandestine operation in Argentina on 21 May, where he was living under the pseudonym Ricardo Klement. By taking this action, Israel effectively stamped its sovereignty and jurisdiction over world Jewry, giving it the legal authority to represent the Jewish people. When Israel's prosecutor Gideon Hausner declared in his opening address at the trial that he speaks for the 'six million' he linked the Holocaust with the State of Israel in a way that had never happened before. This was not about revenge. This was about justice and much more. The entire judicial process proved to be a timely reminder that a powerful and authoritative Israel was guardian of the Jewish people. Now and forever.[17] For Leo and Mina, it was public affirmation, yet again, of Israel's important place in the Jewish world.

The significance of the proceedings went beyond confirming Israel's judicial legitimacy. The Eichmann trial was never just about Eichmann, but predominately about the Holocaust, its victims and, for the first time, its survivors. The trial brought the testimonies of 112 carefully selected witnesses to a world audience.[18] Suddenly they were given centre stage, given a public voice. To a world that had largely remained silent, unmoved by the plight of survivors, their stories were heard and more importantly, listened to. In the world of public opinion their experiences suddenly counted for something. For Leo and Mina who had dedicated years of their lives to the rehabilitation and regeneration of survivors, the Eichmann trial validated all that they had fought so hard to achieve, the right for survivors to live again, to have their place in the world.

Ashdod – A New Industrial City

While the Eichmann trial may have fixated the world, there was still the business of locating Leo's wool tops enterprise. Ashdod, as an industrial centre made very good sense. The city's history, its location and earmarking it as an industrial site was timely and appropriate. Ashdod sat on the Mediterranean coast, 32km south of Tel Aviv and 53km east of Jerusalem. Importantly it was located between Israel's spinning centres in Dimona, Beersheba, Ramat Gan and Petah Tikvah.

The ancient city of Ashdod dates back to the Bronze Age where archaeological findings ironically reveal it as an early textile hub, an export centre of dyed woollen fabrics and garments. By the beginning of the 12th century BCE the city came under the rule of the Philistines, a group of maritime warriors known as the 'Sea People' who wreaked havoc across the Mediterranean. Over the centuries the city was conquered and occupied by the Egyptians, the Persians and the Ancient Greeks. According to the Hebrew bible during the 10th century BCE, Ashdod came under the rule of King David. In 30 BCE it came under the rule of King Herod. In the modern era, during the early 20th century the city was predominately Arab. During the Israeli War of Independence in 1948 the village of 'Isdud' was granted to Israel in the 1949 Armistice Agreements following the end of the war.[19]

The modern city of Ashdod was founded in 1956 on the sand hills near the site of the ancient town. Its first settlers were 22 families from Morocco, followed by a small influx of Egyptian Jews. The city's development was accelerated by Rogosin's substantial investment. The city grew rapidly and by 1961 had a population of 4600. By the early 1960s local and state authorities began to think about developing the town's seafront position. The building of Ashdod Port, the country's largest commercial facility began in 1961 and was inaugurated in 1963. It is the largest port in Israel today, handling 60 per cent of Israel's cargo.[20]

Sixty dunam of what was then sand dunes in Ashdod was acquired by the group of Australian investors led by Leo. It would become the site of the Australian Wool Industries Ltd, the first Australian-owned and operated business in Israel.[21]

Doing Business in Israel

While Israel is now known as the 'start up' nation of the 21st century, a fast moving, innovative and entrepreneurial country, a leader in information technology, medical research and development, the business world of Israel in the early 1960s was not quite so nimble, or quick to act.

In the 1950s and '60s, the socialist philosophy of the main political party in the Israeli Government coalition led to extreme government intervention in the economy. The end result for entrepreneurs like Leo, was a constant stalling of talks, a lack of transparency, having to deal with multiple agencies, and a frustrating amount of time taken to get things done. The bureaucracy was breathtakingly complex. Even for Leo, who was known for his business prowess and for being a tough negotiator, doing business in Israel sorely tested his mettle. And he wasn't the only one frustrated by the conditions by which Israel encouraged investment on the one hand but obstructed its development on the other.

In August 1958, Israel Rogosin gave a scathing account to the *Canadian Jewish Chronicle* of the problems confronting potential investors. Israel's labour costs were too high in relation to its efficiency, Israel's industries were often badly managed, equipped with obsolete machinery and inefficiently run. Water and electricity costs were too high and relied on subsidies. Providing housing and employment for new immigrants was, rightly or wrongly, the country's top priority and took precedence over efficiency and economic productivity. All of this was understandable. But for investors from industrially advanced countries, the difficulties were a tiresome disincentive. But Leo was tenacious, persistent and determined to succeed. Above all, Leo remained motivated by his ideals and not by 'dividends'.[22]

The Australian Wool Industries Ltd

The plant was eventually supported in Israel by the Industrial Development Bank and Bank Leumi. Designed, developed and built by Israeli engineers, architects and building contractors, the mill's machinery was of French, British and Polish origin. Local workers were trained by a small group of experts from South Africa, Poland and Romania, all of whom were brought in to upskill the workforce. Leo oversaw it all. From concept to reality, the entire undertaking took three years. Three long, often difficult, yet exhilarating years.[23]

On 16 May 1963, the official opening of Australian Wool Industries Pty Ltd (AWI) took place. The first all-Australian investment enterprise in Israel – established under the patronage of Pinchas Sapir, was opened in the presence of John Hood CBE, Australian ambassador to Israel. Mina would always proudly refer to the event as 'one of the highlights of our lives'.

Initially the plant employed 100 workers. Its general manager was Australian Israeli Yaacov Feiglin, a chemical engineering graduate of Melbourne University who had spent his formative years in Israel. After a chance meeting in 1962, Leo offered Feiglin the job, deeply impressed with the serious young man who had been offered a position as chemical research director with Israel Mining Industries.[24] In its first year AWI produced 600 tons of wool tops, sales of which amounted to 7 million Israeli pounds (I£). The operation proved profitable and successful. With production in full stride, it became obvious that the local market was limited. A new focus looked towards export markets, notably in Europe and to a lesser extent the Far East. Within a very short time frame and as new markets opened up, the production of wool tops quickly jumped to 2000 tons per annum. As the company grew, demands on Leo increased.[25]

On 16 June 1964 a letter from Feiglin informed Leo 'of a decision of the Executive that Mr Henry Krongold will be devoting time to the affairs of the Company'. The AWI Board sought to divest more of the decision making away from Leo. Regardless of what Leo may have thought about this directive, he supported the board's decisions.[26] He never acted as a one-man band. He was a team player. That was the kind of businessman he was. Leo believed in firm leadership and direction governed by democratic principles and shared responsibilities. By July 1964, Krongold had successfully obtained Israeli Government assurances that would protect the business interests of AWI, but further letters to Leo from Feiglin still revealed 'procrastination' on Israel's part.[27]

Yet, the company continued to profit. In an article in the *Jerusalem Post* in December 1964, the Australian operation was lauded. It highlighted three advantages of the enterprise: its model up-to-date industrial plant, its ability to produce a natural product good for export and import opportunities, and its ability to act as a bridgehead for fostering economic ties between Israel and Australia. All were objectives that Leo had set out to achieve. All were reached.

In 1965 Leo and Mina returned to Australia after dividing much of their time for the past five years between their two homes, in Tel Aviv and Melbourne. It was then that Leo's leading role with AWI came to an end. Leo no longer saw eye to eye with the board of AWI. There were differences of opinion in how the company should be run both from Australia and within Israel, 'industry in Israel is more political than economic' he bemoaned. There was a clash of ideals and person-alities, all of which forced Leo to relinquish his chairmanship of the Australian Wool Industries. The board elected Henry Krongold as chairman in 1965. Regardless of differences, Leo remained an investor and a supporter of the enterprise.[28]

Leo remained totally committed to the economic bridge that had been built between Israel and Australia. From 31 March until 4 April 1968, on the personal invitation of Israel's prime minister Levi Eshkol, Leo and Mina attended the first Israel Economic Conference in Jerusalem, convened by Eshkol. Leo was a leader of the Australian delegation, another point of great pride for both Leo and Mina.[29]

Throughout 1968 and 1969, following a resolution taken at the Israel Economic Conference, Leo attempted to establish an Australian–Israeli Chamber of Commerce. He had hoped to promote and market Israeli products in Australia but felt thwarted by what he called the 'Zionist establishment' whom he believed controlled the agenda and 'who look upon Israel, rightly or wrongly, as their private property and resent any initiative which does not bear the Zionist label and is not controlled by the bosses of the establishment'. The Melbourne Jewish community was political and highly factionalised. Leo knew this and played his part in it, but always to the advancement of the community. He could see beyond the party politics.[30]

Australian Wool Industries continued to operate profitably throughout the 1960s and most of the 1970s, with sales reaching I₤50 million in 1972. But following the Yom Kippur war in 1973, a breakdown of the shipping route between Israel and Australia, as well as a subsequent fall in demand and falling prices, the company experienced unsustainable, serious financial loss. The Australian shareholding group decided to pull out. Between February and March 1978 their shares were bought out by the Polgat Woollen Industries, Kiryat Gat, Ptd Ltd, effectively ending AWI as an Australian entity.[31]

Back to Business in Melbourne

Throughout the remainder of the 1960s and at the start of the 1970s, in Leo's last years, he returned to those matters which were close to his heart and remained front of mind. His focus never strayed far from Jewish Welfare, remaining a figurehead for the organisation and being instrumental in its fundraising initiatives. Leo retained a significant interest in the Fink family business, overseeing some of its expansion. He and Mina gave generously to their many philanthropic interests, while Leo remained a vocal public figure on matters that challenged his ideals and stirred his passions.

Leo's counsel was sought by Walter Lippmann, president of the Australian Jewish Welfare and Relief Society, when Leo was asked to be chairman of the Immigration Section of the program at the AJWRS conference on 28–31 January 1965. On 13 August 1965 Leo was again asked to be chairman of the Special Gifts Division of the

AJWRS Annual Appeal. His role involved managing major donors, a task he undertook with considerable success. So much so that again in 1970 Leo was asked by Kalman Rogers who was then president of the AJWRS Annual Appeal, to assist in canvassing and collecting major donations. Again, his success in soliciting large gifts, was noted. 'Leo was a hard man to refuse'.[32]

In 1967 the Fink brothers purchased 'Castlemaine Woollen Mills' while the business was in receivership. On 9 April 1970, *The Age* publicised that 'Fink Carpets group to go public' and to float the company. The paper also announced that a $4 million nylon plant was to open by the end of the year in Thomastown, Victoria. Leo enjoyed expanding the business. It brought him back to his family roots.

Leo's connection with his cultural heritage remained strong. The former immigrant from Bialystok retained an interest in and commitment to perpetuating Yiddish culture and to supporting its writers. In mid-1970 Leo was instrumental in the establishment of the 'Herz Bergner Memorial Fund' to support the publication of books by Jewish writers. An avid reader and book collector, Leo was regularly approached to give financial assistance to struggling writers. He rarely, if ever, refused. In August 1972 Leo contributed $1000 towards the publication of Moshe Ajzenbud's next Yiddish publication.[33]

In May 1972, Leo and Mina gave a $10,000 donation to the new building costs of the Kadimah, now located in Elsternwick. Sender Burstin, a long-time friend, who had been a co- welfare worker in those heady post-war years and now a himself a leader of the Kadimah, wrote to inform them that the main Kadimah hall would be named in Leo's honour. In November 1972 the main hall of the new building was named 'The Leo Fink Hall'. A fitting tribute, one that would stand the test of time.

Leo never hesitated to make his views and opinions known to politicians and community leaders. Prime ministers, leaders of the opposition, state premiers all would hear from Leo if the occasion presented itself. On 1 May 1972, Leo penned a personal letter to Sir Henry Bolte, premier of Victoria, congratulating him on his handling of the TNT dispute and The Holding Student demonstration. 'Tackle your opposition with mercy but remain on the winning side', he advised. It was a teaching on life itself, a mantra by which Leo fearlessly lived.[34]

He would freely give his opinion to those running Jewish Welfare. In August 1972 he cautioned Walter Lippmann against getting involved in matters unrelated to Jewish Welfare, in this case the crisis confronting Indian citizens of Uganda forced to flee the dictatorship of Idi Amin. He warned Lippmann to stick to his core business. 'You are forgetting Walter', he wrote, 'you are now the President of the Welfare Society and Federation of Welfare Societies. You represent a community of middle-class Jews ... your first loyalty should be to them ... I value your devotion to the community. I would hate to see you on the defensive. Stay out of trouble'. He also cautioned a young, newly employed social worker, Lionel Sharpe, against discarding volunteers in Jewish Welfare in favour of paid employees, strongly believing that volunteers gave more than their time, but integrated important elements of the community and most importantly its spirit, a spirit that could not be bought. Leo and Mina's work bore testament to that.[35]

A Pioneer to the End

Leo was plagued with ill health in the last couple of years of his life. After a battle with brain cancer, Leo passed away on 20 September 1972, on his and Mina's 40th wedding anniversary. He was 71 years of age. Leo remained active and engaged until the end, corresponding with colleagues, community leaders and, as time ran out, particularly with his rabbi. The day before he died, Leo penned a reflective piece to the Kew congregation's Rabbi Schreiber. There was no bitterness, no rancour, but an appreciation for all that was good in his life.

> I understood the concept of fate and the symbolic, mystic and religious meaning of destiny. Life must go on and I carry on to the best of my ability. How wonderful it is for one to carry on normally, to think clearly and not to lose faith. I am lucky that I am surrounded by so much love and attention by my wife and family.[36]

Leo left behind a 59-year-old grieving widow, two married children and six grandchildren.

The family received an overwhelming number of condolences from politicians on both sides of the political divide, business leaders, community leaders, a vast extended family and a multitude of friends and colleagues, here and overseas. Obituaries were written. The *Australian Jewish News* highlighted Leo's particular humanitarian vision, one that sought to give individuals the means to be independent and self-sufficient. 'Leo was unique in his generation – an industrialist and an intellectual, who believed that the unfortunate of the world were entitled not to charity but to the means for their own rehabilitation.'[37] Tributes were delivered. Benzion Patkin, a long-time friend and colleague, emphasised Leo's vigour and creativity, 'when an idea crystallized in his mind, he did not rest until it was realized … his energy and initiative had no limits'.[38] Commemorative evenings were held where hundreds came to pay their respects and pay homage to a life lived exceptionally well, a life devoted to the service of others. Leo was a man who had left his mark.

The official opening of Melbourne's 'Leo Fink Court', 26 flats for the aged at 27 Fulton Street in East St Kilda, took place on 20 May 1973. The Hon. Bill Hayden, minister for social security, presided, Walter Lippmann did the 'welcome' and Sydney Einfeld, president of the Federation of Australian Jewish Welfare Societies, delivered the keynote address. Providing housing for the aged and infirm, helping others less fortunate to still believe in a future, would have met with Leo's approval.

Leo's legacy, his pioneering spirit, is best summed up in the eulogy that was delivered by Rabbi Schreiber. 'It was his historic privilege to become and to remain a Jewish pioneer who used the best of yesterday for the upbuilding of the Jewish tomorrow.'[39]

Mina never remarried. She never re-partnered. Mina continued the course that she and Leo had set for themselves, to ensure that there would be a 'Jewish tomorrow'. The Jewish world did not stand still and neither did Mina.

Chapter 10

BEING MINA

Mina Fink was proud to call herself a feminist. But she wasn't the bra burning type. Her brand of feminism stemmed from her prevailing sense of what was just, fair and equitable. This was how she was raised. This was how she was educated. This was the life she had lived for 40 years with her beloved Leo, the man who gave her all the opportunities she needed to step up and be the person she could be. 'He provided me with a lesson in life', Mina recalled many years later.[1] While Leo had been her great enabler, giving her the encouragement, economic security and social stability she needed, what Mina brought to the table was a powerful self-belief in her own ability. She never considered herself anything but anyone's equal. All she asked for was that men do the same. 'Men were inclined to think that women were there to "make the tea", and really I don't see why they shouldn't make the tea for us, sometimes ...', Mina told a newspaper reporter.[2]

After spending several years in Israel supporting Leo in his develop-ment of the Israel venture, Mina was ready for a new challenge. Not that she didn't enjoy her time in Israel. She revelled in it. While there, she learnt Hebrew at 'ulpan' classes, cultivated a wide circle of friends, proved yet again that she was the consummate hostess, and enjoyed social networking, a skill she was particularly good at and which always served her well. But the times, as Bob Dylan told us in 1964, were 'a-Changin''.

Four years before Leo's passing, Mina stepped into a new, far-reaching leadership role. On 19 June 1967, Mina was elected national president of the National Council of Jewish Women (NCJW), an organisation she had served as Victorian president from 1957 to 1960. But this time Mina had found a new voice, as head of an organisation that was now in need of an 'ideological make over'.[3] Mina inherited a NCJW steeped in a three-point platform of national work for Israel and state work for local Jewish and non-Jewish causes.[4] Mina did not abandon these ideals, and in her first editorial in *The Council Bulletin* as national president, she called for a continued commitment to 'Israel, The Community and Humanity'.[5] But Mina was alert to the sweeping social changes taking place around her, subsequently her focus increasingly shifted to women's affairs and the international scene.

Over her six-year presidency Mina reshaped and reinvigorated the organisation at every level. Her presidency moved the NCJW headquarters from Sydney to Melbourne, for the first time in 44 years. Mina was the NCJW's first Polish-born Yiddish-speaking president. It was a role that suited her expansive vision, global reach and impeccable networking skills. Mina believed that in serving the international needs of Jewish women she could affect greater, more lasting change.

Mina's time at the helm of the NCJW was a defining period for her, the organisation she led and the world in which she lived.

The 1960s – The Move Towards Internationalism

While the 1950s was a time when Australians began discovering themselves, the 1960s in Australia was a period of accelerating and exhilarating social change, from which a more outward looking society emerged. This change was underscored by a buoyant economy, a prosperous middle class and the coming of age of a generation of 'baby boomers' seen as champions of political protest and sexual freedom. The 1960s was a transitional decade that challenged the conservative elements of the 1950s and brought with it a new sense of internationalism, diminished attachment to the British Commonwealth and a new alignment with American and European popular culture and politics. In 1967 the word 'British' was removed from Australian passports. Australia was modernising itself, more accepting of change and the effects of increased, affordable travel, new technologies and non-British migration. This 'cosmopolitan influence', a term coined by Australian writer George Johnston in 1966, was largely a result of post-war migration that helped catapult Australia into a new, more ethnically diverse era.[6] Mina had always considered herself a citizen of the world, a member of a global community. Now it was Australia's turn.

Just two weeks before Mina stepped into her national NCJW role, Israel, for the third time in its short existence, was bracing itself for the fight of its life. In the lead up to the 'Six Day War', the existential threat the Arab world posed to Jewish life in Israel, the fear of an imminent second Holocaust, shook Australian Jewry to the core. Mina was no exception. Israel launched a pre-emptive attack against its enemies on 5 June 1967 and within six days had vanquished the Arab armies that had threatened to 'wipe Israel off the map'.[7] Fundraising went into overdrive. One of the first things Mina did in her presidency was to immediately announce that a cheque for $4000, representing years of savings for much-longed-for council premises, was handed over to the Israel Emergency Appeal. 'We are only too happy to dig into our humble reserves and give it', Mina recorded in her incoming president's report.[8]

At a time of growing dissent and disillusionment over Australia's involvement in the Vietnam War, with an increasing number of anti-Vietnam rallies protesting against a war many Australians saw as unjust and unnecessary, the Six Day War was seen as a moral war, a David and Goliath battle. The mainstream press saw Israel as the underdog, the Israeli soldiers as 'unsung heroes'.[9]

From 31 May to 4 June 1968, Mina was again in Israel, this time as chairman of Resolutions at the International Council of Jewish Women's (ICJW) Triennial Conference in what was now a Jerusalem that included the sacred Jewish sites of the Old City, sites she had previously been unable to visit. Established in 1912, the International Council of Jewish Women (ICJW) was formed as an umbrella organisation representing Jewish women and women's organisations, now extending to 34 member countries. At the 1968 conference, NCJW Australia supported the consolidation of projects in Israeli agriculture, housing and education, for the 'benefit of Israel and the whole world'.

The 1970s – Changes and Challenges

The 1970s brought the feminist agenda into the mainstream. What was termed the 'women's rights movement' or more generally the 'women's liberation movement' was a 'diverse social movement of the 1960s and '70s that sought equal rights, opportunities and greater personal freedom for women. It coincided with and is recognised as part of the 'second wave' of feminism. While the first-wave feminism of the 19th and early 20th centuries focused on women's legal rights, especially the right to vote, the 'second-wave' women's rights movement touched on every area of women's experience – including politics, work, the family and sexuality'.[10]

Mina was no radical revolutionary, but she was a woman of the times. She quickly grasped the enormous changes that were taking place for women and the flow on effects for the women's movement and non-profit organisations. While Mina identified as a feminist, she did not see the role of women supplanting men. Mina believed that women had an important place in the wider world without abrogating their pivotal role in family life. All she sought to do was to 'extend their influence', to ensure that their voices were heard and their efforts rewarded equitably.

Mina also believed that the race for equality was one that had to be run and shared with the men. 'We are almost there in this equality battle', she told a newspaper reporter in 1970. 'What we need now, to bridge the gap, is the help of the men, and the women must seek this help'.[11] In two short years Mina's plea to 'bridge the gap' came in the form of a political thunderbolt.

Political Change and Social Reform

In 1972 the Whitlam Labor government was swept to power on the promise of major social reform. It was the first federal Labor government to hold office since Ben Chifley lost the 1949 election. 'It's time' was the Labor party catchcry, one that resonated with a country hungry for change. Amongst its many plans, the government immediately brought in a raft of reforms designed to eradicate discrimination against women. Equal pay for men and women saw a million female workers become eligible for full pay, with an overall increase in women's wages of approximately 30 per cent. The luxury tax was abolished on all contraceptives and the pill was put on the National Health Scheme list. The federal *Child Care Act 1972* was passed providing funded child care facilities for sick or working parents. Family day care, after school care and playgroups soon followed. The Supporting Mother's Benefit gave financial assistance to single mothers who were not eligible for the widow's pension. This reform had a profound impact on the child adoption program as it gave single mothers the option to be self-supporting. In doing so it reduced the number of children available for adoption. In 1973 Commonwealth female public servants were granted paid maternity leave for 12 weeks and unpaid leave up to 40 weeks.

In 1975 under the Fraser Liberal government the *Family Law Act* established the principle of no-fault divorce in Australian law. 'No-fault' means that a court does not consider which partner was at fault in the marriage breakdown. This meant that women could file for no-fault divorce. In the same year Dame Margaret Guilfoyle became the first woman to be appointed to the Federal Cabinet as a minister. She held the Education and Social Service portfolio. In 1977 the Victorian *Equal Opportunity Act* created the Equal Opportunity Board and the Office of Equal Opportunity Commissioner. The Act outlawed discrimination based on marital status and gender in employment, education, accommodation and provision of goods and services.[12]

Interestingly, none of these reforms had any direct impact on Mina's personal life. They did not change the way she lived. Leo had ensured that Mina was well provided for. But they profoundly changed the social landscape and the personal fortunes of millions of other women. It signalled a move towards equality and parity that Mina wholeheartedly supported. Women were the direct beneficiaries of social and political reforms that were legislated and passed into law with 'the help of men'. Just as Mina had envisaged.

Mina's NCJW Grassroots Revolution

Mina believed that the future and longevity of any organisation relied on its capacity to renew itself. This centred on her belief that organisations would only survive if they remained relevant, addressing the needs of the times. That meant being receptive to change, resilient and adaptable, traits that were reflected in Mina herself.

Following the lengthy presidencies of Fanny Reading and Vera Cohen, Mina felt that the national presidency should be limited to six years and the seat of NCJW government be alternated between Melbourne and Sydney. Sylvia Gelman succeeded Mina as national president in 1973. The constitution then changed to reflect limited tenure and alternating location. This avoided stagnation and ensured renewal and regrowth.[13]

Mina was greatly influenced by the methodology and energy of the American NCJW, she was impressed with the number and calibre of highly educated younger women who took on leadership roles. Consequently, Mina actively sought to engage an educated younger generation of women in taking on leadership roles in Australia. In this way the organisation would constantly be reinvigorated.

Women who had skills in writing, public speaking and organising were conscripted into Mina's 'new' army. Mina's drive to recruit young dynamic women bore fruit. A young Zelda Rosenbaum, who would later spearhead the Jewish Museum in Melbourne was recruited by Mina to organise an exhibition of Judaica at the Victorian Art Gallery as part of the 1975 ICJW Convention. When the United Nations Assembly proclaimed 1975 International Year for Women, the federal government under Gough Whitlam set up a raft of activities and programs with significant funding, in excess of $3 million, to ensure its success.

In the same year the NCJW delegation to the Australian International Year for Women Committee, convened by Elizabeth Reid, special advisor to the prime minister on women's issues, was headed by the dynamic young mother and lawyer Ada Moshinsky, a future QC.[14]

Mina's younger talented protégés included the future leaders of NCJW; Sylvia Gelman, who recalled being 'coaxed, cajoled, and sometimes subtly coerced' by Mina, Geulah Solomon who extolled Mina as a 'brilliant leader and activist on behalf of our community' and Malvina Malinek who owed her 'involvement in NCJW, ICJW and the community to Mina'.[15] But she also brought along others who had the knowledge to guide and assist. Her ability to enlist family and former co-workers from her Jewish Welfare days included Sadie Fink, Eva Joel, and Annia Castan, who later wrote to Mina thanking her for her ongoing advice and support. 'You are the ideas woman who can see the potential in a person. Thank you for your confidence in me'.[16] It was a sentiment shared by many of Mina's loyal co-workers and friends. Mina believed that the strength of any organisation lay in a healthy mix of new talent, new ideas and hardened experience.

Mina also imparted a new professionalism in the running of meetings and fundraising, skills she had honed in her days leading the Ladies' Group of Jewish Welfare. Accurate record keeping and correct procedures were crucial to running a professional organisation and Mina never lost her zest for enforcing strict protocols.

Mina harboured a dream to establish the NCJW's own premises in Melbourne as it had in Sydney. Together with Malvina Malinek, she organised the Trust Foundation, which generated funds for the Victorian Section's philanthropic endeavours. Working with her sister-in-law, Sadie Fink, the foundation rolled over the profits from the International Council of Jewish Women (ICJW) Convention into a fund for the establishment of the Victorian Section's Council House. When the deposit on the NCJW's first modest property in Westbury Street was put down in 1980, the dream became a reality.[17] By 1982 NCJW had outgrown this property. It was sold and new premises were bought in Hawthorn Road, Caulfield. Mina Fink's 'Family Foundation' supported the purchase of rooms at this property while Sadie Fink and Annia Castan bought the shop next door which was converted into a function room.[18]

Israel, Humanitarianism, Human Rights Advocacy

Mina advanced the organisation into a humanitarian, global role. As a result of her attendance at the international conventions of the ICJW in 1954, 1963, 1966, 1969, Mina initiated large-scale international projects that really put the NCJW on the map.

Her attendance at the 1969 conference in Israel was highlighted by a special dedication ceremony held at Moshav Alma, situated seven kilometres from the Lebanon border in the upper Galilee. The Alma project was originally adopted by the NCJW under the urging of Fanny Reading and Vera Cohen in 1966. The Australian NCJW supported the building of a synagogue and community centre. With Mina in attendance the NCJW made a presentation of four scholarships to the *moshav* (communal agricultural settlement). 'The children sang "my bonny lies over the ocean" which they prepared in English specially for us', Mina proudly recalled.[19]

In June 1970 Mina as NCJW national president, announced that the Council would join with all major Australian women's organis- ations to build a $200,000 women students' hall of residence at the University of Papua New Guinea.[20] It was a major NCJW contribution towards the International Education Year, called by the United Nations to encourage countries to do 'something extra or special about their educational problems'. This spoke to the heart of Mina who highly valued education and saw it as a means of lifting women out of poverty and inequality. For Mina this project was about expansion, 'accepting additional responsibilities without diverting funds from one cause to another'.[21]

An unfair Jewish divorce law which gave men the authority to withhold a religious divorce, a 'gett', from the wife indefinitely, was also targeted by NCJW. It was a law that meant women were unable to remarry in a religious ceremony if the former husband refused. In 1970 Mina told the *Courier Mail* that a petition was signed by NCJW as part of an international movement which represented more than one million Jewish women throughout the world.[22] The petition was forwarded by the ICJW to the chief rabbis of Israel, Unterman and Nissim, requesting a reinterpretation of Jewish law so that it could constructively deal with divorce, desertion and *chalitzah*, the process by which a childless widow and a brother of her deceased husband may avoid the duty to marry. It was a show of strength and solidarity. It was about speaking out for women who had no public voice. It was about bringing the might of the women's movement into action.

Although no longer president in 1975, Mina took on the role of chair at the ICJW's 10th Triennial Convention in Australia. It was a conference she and Sylvia Gelman had lobbied to have in Melbourne. This was the first international meeting to be held in Australia by any Jewish organisation. It profiled the work of the NCJW and its role in world affairs. Twenty delegates from the United Kingdom, plus members from Latin America, France, South Africa and New Zealand gathered in Melbourne under the coordination of Mina Fink, Sadie Fink and Sylvia Gelman. Profits from the sale of the convention brochure also went towards the purchase of the Council house in Westbury Street, East St Kilda.

In the same year, the *Woman's Day* wrote an article about women's organisations around the world that had quietly been activists and advocates for the empowerment and advancement of women long before 'women's liberation' had ever been spoken of. It singled out six women, one of whom was Mina Fink.[23]

The NCJW minutes of 27 May 1980 recorded that, as international vice president of ICJW, Mina was actively involved in the campaign to free Soviet 'refusenik' Ida Nudel, imprisoned and sentenced to four years of 'internal' exile in a Siberian labour camp, for the 'crime' of applying for a visa to leave the Soviet Union for Israel.[24] It was Mina who led a protest delegation of NCJW members to the Russian embassy in Canberra. Nudel was released from Siberia in 1982, then 'permitted' to live for five years in Moldova. In 1987 she was granted an exit visa to Israel. Mina was both courageous and fearless in campaigning against antisemitism and its newer incarnation, anti-Zionism.

The Fight Against the 'Zionism is Racism' UN Resolution

By the time Mina relinquished her NCJW national presidency in 1973, Israel was no longer viewed as the underdog fighting a David and Goliath battle, but as an aggressor, an occupier of stolen land, an oppressor of the Palestinian people. The wheel of public opinion had quickly turned. In 1975 the United Nations declared an International Year for Women. As a result, an international conference was held in Mexico. The Australian delegation included Elizabeth Reid, Margaret Whitlam and Susan Ryan. Jewish and non-Jewish women's organisations embraced the idea of such a conference and looked forward to working together on poverty and injustice. However, the Mexico conference took the opportunity for the first time to categorise Zionism as a form of racism. 'Zionism is Racism' United Nations General Assembly Resolution 3379, was formally adopted by the UN later that year. It was a bitter setback for Jewish organisations that wanted to keep divisive politics out of the realm of international social action programs.[25]

The UN's Peak Council of National Women's Non-Government Organisations organised another conference in Copenhagen in 1980. This time Mina and Sylvia Gelman wanted to be prepared. They led a delegation to meet with Andrew Peacock, then minister for foreign affairs, to protest against the singling out of Palestinian women being on the agenda to the exclusion of all other women. The delegation was assured that the Australian Government would vote for an amendment of the resolution.[26] The Copenhagen delegation of 15 women representing the Australian Government and five non-government women tried to remain non-antagonistic. Together with the USA, Canada and Israel, they voted against the resolutions equating Zionism with racism. But it was clear the conference agenda had been hijacked. Rather than lead a broad discussion based on women's needs, terrorists such as Leila Khaled were given a platform to promote their view that Zionism equates to racism. Mina enlisted a young Eve Mahlab to be a participant at Copenhagen and to try to counter the damning 'Zionism is Racism' United Nations resolution. Once the contentious resolution was endorsed by the UN, it became difficult to counter. The NCJW wanted to remain non-political and did not want to be seen as a lobby group but this struck at the core of their beliefs.

At the NCJW conference on the Gold Coast in 1982 Mina pressed for stronger Israel advocacy, a grassroots way of putting Israel's case forward in an informed, constructive manner. Mina believed that NCJW members could advance Israel's cause, but in doing so had to be educated in order to counter anti-Israel commentary. She recommended that all branches of the NCJW subscribe to the *Jerusalem Post* and the *Australia/Israel Review*.[27]

At the UN Decade for Women Conference in Nairobi in 1985, as a result of representations made by the NCJW in collaboration with the Women's International Zionist Organization (WIZO), the Australian delegation refrained from endorsing resolutions which stipulated that Zionism equates to racism.[28] This was a considerable achievement. The infamous UN resolution was not rescinded until 1991.

Mina's unflinching advocacy for Israel and the Jewish world would continue for the remainder of her life. She spent lengthy periods of time in Israel, they were 'amongst the happiest times of my life' she would often tell friends. Her grandchildren formed strong attachments to Israel. Many lived there intermittently, many studied there, or made *aliyah*. Several of them married there. Mina was always the proud grandmother in attendance.

Mina's support for Israel's public institutions was unequivocal. On 13 July 1984, she became a 'Guardian' of the Western Pacific Friends of Beit Hatfutsot at the Museum of the Diaspora in Tel Aviv, a title bestowed on significant donors.[29] Due to the vision and support of the president of the World Jewish Congress, Nahum Goldman, the museum was founded in 1978 and situated in the heart of the Tel Aviv University campus in Ramat Aviv. The museum tells the enduring cultural and religious story of the Jewish people, in a way that is accessible to people of all faiths. Mina's financial backing was testament to her belief in the importance of Jewish education. For her, education was the gateway to Jewish continuity. It fostered a greater understanding and acceptance of the diversity and richness of Jewish life. In 2005, the Israeli Knesset passed the 'Beit Hatfutsot Law' that defines Beit Hatfutsot as 'the National Centre for Jewish communities in Israel and around the world'.[30]

In line with her interest in supporting tertiary education, in June 1985 Mina made a generous donation of $10,000 to the Golda Meir Fellowship at the Hebrew University of Jerusalem. Mina always regretted never having attended university. This was a way of ensuring others did not miss out on an opportunity for further study. Established in 1984, the Golda Meir Fellowship Fund was designed to attract scholars of outstanding academic achievement from all parts of the world, including Israel, and enable them to pursue post-doctoral studies in a range of disciplines at the Hebrew University of Jerusalem.[31]

Reward for Effort

On 1 January 1974 Mina was awarded the MBE – Member of the British Empire 'in recognition of her long and outstanding community service, particularly in the interests of Jewish Women'. Mina was proud of the award, not out of personal vanity, although she enjoyed the high profile that came with a public life, but rather because it was an act of recognition and respect. Her son Nathan recalled in a 2002 public address that 'respectability; that was very important to her. She liked to be invited to Government House, to the Royal Ball, to be introduced to prime ministers, ambassadors and governors. The Finks thought that was all nonsense, but to her it spelt recognition'.[32]

Mina's involvement with the Lady Mayoress Committee also brought with it status and recognition. Founded in 1959 the Lady Mayoress Committee was a non-profit organisation dedicated to raising awareness and funds for various projects that assisted children and women in need, a focus that resonated with Mina, who enjoyed a style of fundraising that involved high teas, luncheons, raffles and unwavering support for the Royal Family. Being on the committee highlighted her willingness to be involved with non-Jewish organisations that served the needs of the underprivileged. It also brought her into contact with a range of high-profile individuals, all of whom became part of Mina's ever-expanding social network.

In 1987 Mina was elected vice president of the International Council of Jewish Women and made an Honorary Life Member of the ICJW's executive, an honour she relished and which also signalled recognition for the efforts she had undertaken and achievements reached at a national and international level.

An Enduring Commitment to Jewish Welfare

While Mina developed her interest in women's affairs and as her leadership role within the NCJW soared, her commitment to Jewish Welfare remained undiminished. Even after Leo's passing, she continued as an active and vocal director on the board of the Australian Jewish Welfare and Relief Society (AJWRS). When her official role on the AJWRS Board ended in 1977, her link to the organisation that she and Leo had spearheaded and that was responsible for resettling thousands of Holocaust survivors continued. Her ties to Jewish Welfare remained strong and unbreakable. But the role the AJWRS played in the community and the direction it took had changed. The manner in which it operated had too. Again, Mina moved with the times.

Walter Lippmann was president of the AJWRS until 1977. Under his leadership, the organisation continued to professionalise its operations, relying more and more on evidence-based research in its decision making and to guide its future direction. This led Walter to personally undertake a number of demographic research projects including detailed analyses of the 1961 and 1966 censuses and a 1969 paper on 'Marriage patterns in the Melbourne Jewish community'. Although self-taught, Walter's work was recognised for its importance in informing the community of demographic trends. The ageing of the community, the community's low birth rate and the rate of intermarriage were key challenges that Walter believed required concerted communal action and diligent planning.[33]

Throughout the 1960s a spate of research activities in the Melbourne Jewish community saw the involvement of major figures in Jewish research, Ron Taft and Peter Medding, both of whom undertook exploratory surveys in Melbourne that set a benchmark for work of this kind and which have stood the test of time. Mina was extremely supportive of this line of investigation. A professional approach was in keeping with her own standards. She financially sponsored a number of academic investigations, including Ron Taft's contribution to 'Jews in Australian Society', a collection of academic essays edited by Peter Medding and published in 1973 and a student scholarship provided through Jewish Welfare to David Brous for a Master's thesis examining 'Jewish Immigration into Australia 1920–1950', completed in 1976. Mina welcomed an informed historical perspective being incorporated into the public record, particularly if it acknowledged Leo's considerable achievements. Rigorous study and academic research also ensured an accurate retelling of the past. All of which Mina wholeheartedly endorsed.

But some things never change. While research now played a part in the AJWRS's crucial decision making, the financial needs of the community remained great. Jewish Welfare's communal role still depended on active fundraising and in this Mina continued to play her considerable part.

In September 1976, Mina was nominated as Appeal patron for AJWRS with a target of $300,000. It was a role she understood well. Welfare was an intrinsic part of Jewish life and it required constant communal support. 'Helping and welfare is not a new concept to the Jews; it is part and parcel of our tradition and religion. With almost every new settlement, a simultaneous growth with the synagogue was a welfare organisation', she said at the opening of the Appeal on 19 September. 'There was a misconception', Mina added, 'of Jews and non-Jews who believed the Jewish community was a society of the rich, without need for a welfare organisation'.[34] Mina reiterated that Jews helping other Jews was still the only way to survive. 'If we don't look after ourselves, who then can we rely on?'[35]

On 1 August 1985, the then president of the AJWRS Rodney Benjamin approached Mina to again be Appeal patron. 'Your association with the 1985 Appeal will assist us in realising our much increased, but very necessary target for 1985/6.' She accepted Benjamin's request and led the campaign, keen to assist with the organisation's new programs for the aged and children with disability. Mina did not see her role as ceremonial; she actively sought donations and played a role in planning and hosting events.[36]

In 1987 Mina was approached again to be president of the AJWRS Appeal. The Appeal had the most ambitious objective yet, to raise 'one million dollars plus'. Mina led the campaign team and was assisted by John Gandel as Appeal patron, Liesel Adler and Walter Jona as vice presidents, Geoffrey Green as chairman, Rodney Benjamin and Mina's son Nathan Fink as treasurers. Her team was formidable. Mina pledged 'to do all in my power to make the Appeal the success it deserves'.[37]

Mina's sense of mission, her 'sacred obligation' to serve the needs of others was expressed in her opening 1987 Appeal address. 'We have a sacred obligation to maintain and if necessary, extend the services for the aged, for the young, for the physically and mentally handicapped. I have every confidence that the community will respond to the Appeal as they have done in the past, with their hearts and pockets.'[38]

By the 1980s Mina, the modern feminist, Israel advocate and devoted charity worker, was in her seventies. She had demonstrated continued, unswerving dedication towards the NCJW and the AJWRS, both in her official and unofficial capacity. She could have made the decision to sit back, to look no further, to be content with her achievements, to enjoy her family and friends, her walks in the Botanical gardens. After all, she had given of herself to the worthiest of causes. But there was one more cause that she could not ignore, one more campaign that pushed her back to where it all began; the Holocaust. Mina had unfinished business.

Chapter 11

BACK TO THE
HOLOCAUST

Holocaust survivor Sheva Glas-Wiener had an important story to tell. Not of her own miraculous survival. That would have been enough. Death camp Auschwitz, the slave labour camp of Jesau by Königsberg and concentration camp Stutthof, situated in the swampy, dense woodlands just south of Danzig, she survived them all. In the last days of the war, with the Nazis in retreat, a parting 'gift' was given to the remaining Stutthof survivors. Sheva and hundreds of others were herded onto a cargo ship laden with explosives in the Baltic Sea. Crammed into the ship's filthy rat-infested hold without food and little water, Sheva remained there for three weeks. When the ship came under heavy air attack from Allied bombers unaware of its human cargo, it exploded into a ball of fire. Most drowned or were burnt alive. Surrounded by bodies in flames, with her own clothes on fire, she jumped into the ocean. A handful of survivors were picked up by another ship. Sheva was one of them. She survived that too. But there was another story that would not let her rest, the memories that tore at her heart and tortured her soul. A story of orphaned children who did not survive, 1600 innocent children who were murdered in 1942. This was the story that Sheva Glas-Wiener knew she had to tell. And it was a story that Mina Fink was determined the world would know.[1]

Before the outbreak of war, Sheva's home town of Lodz was a wealthy, industrial powerhouse, Poland's second-largest city, with a Jewish population of 230,000. The German invasion of Poland began on 1 September 1939. Within one-week Lodz was defeated and occupied. Nazi rule brought immediate death, destruction and homelessness. Many fled the city. Some managed to escape to regions not yet occupied, others were caught, imprisoned or shot. The Jewish welfare society of Lodz, particularly moved by the plight of orphans left to roam the streets and beg for scraps of food, managed to secure various makeshift accommodations for thousands of destitute children. The Children's Colony of Marysin, on the outskirts of Lodz, was among them.[2]

In 1940, Sheva Glas-Wiener was a 22-year-old teacher assigned to care for these children and supervise their education. The orphanage was housed in a number of dwellings, dilapidated weatherboard houses and straw-roofed huts, devoid of sewerage or heating, with only the most basic amenities. The orphanage became a small self-contained community, staffed by dedicated guardians and devoted teachers like Sheva who did all in their power to create a home for their destitute charges. The Marysin orphanage was fenced off by barbed wire, patrolled and guarded by armed German soldiers.[3]

The orphanage came under the jurisdiction of the Lodz ghetto, a ghetto whose walls were sealed off from the world on 1 May 1940. Any contact with neighbouring Poles or the underground was shut down due the city's annexation into the Third Reich and the total subjugation of the Polish population. In other ghettos such as Warsaw, Krakow or Lublin, where limited interaction with the Poles was possible, some children had been smuggled out and hidden, but not in Lodz. The

Jews of the Lodz ghetto were completely isolated, cut off as nowhere else. No one got in or out.[4]

The number of ghetto inhabitants peaked at a staggering 164,000. All were confined within a four-square-kilometre area in the already overcrowded, teeming slums of Baluty and the Old City, the poorest part of town. The ghetto's mortality rate was high; epidemics, especially typhus, were rampant. Ghetto documents record that 43,500 people died of starvation, cold or disease. Of the rest, the vast majority were murdered. Sheva's family was among them. By war's end on 8 May 1945, only about 8000 of the ghetto's inmates remained alive. Orphaned children, some of the most vulnerable and disadvantaged of the ghetto dwellers, didn't stand a chance.[5]

Of the 1600 impoverished children housed in the Marysin orphanage, 32 girls, aged between 7 and 15, were Sheva's direct responsibility. From 1940 to 1942 Sheva spent every waking hour with these 32 children, under the same inhumane, brutal conditions, suffering the same starvation and disease as the ghetto inhabitants. Some of these children came from the slums of Lodz, others came from prosperous, middle-class Jewish homes in Berlin, Vienna or Prague, left destitute after their parents were rounded up and deported. Sheva became their surrogate mother, was privy to their hopes and aspirations. Above all, she bore witness to their common humanity, their desperate will to live. She was also witness to their deaths.[6] In 1942, when the ghetto order came to 'give up the children', to prepare them for their final journey, Sheva was helpless.[7] On 9 September 1942, she watched as all the children were led away to the train station, many shot or beaten before they could board the cattle car that took them to Chelmno, a two-hour trip from Lodz, where the gas vans stood waiting.[8]

It wasn't until 1970, after the passage of time had brought some healing, that Sheva put pen to paper, to fulfil a commitment she had made to herself and to the children. She would write their story. It was fitting that the story was first written in Yiddish, the language spoken by many of the children and the language closest to Sheva, who had in her early years been an accomplished writer and poet of Polish and Yiddish stories. For Sheva, this was not just about how they died, but more importantly how they lived. She made a conscious decision to write about their daily lives, how they sought comfort and love amongst each other, how they played their childish games amidst the dirt and squalor, how they strove to diligently learn their lessons each day. She was always touched by the songs they would joyfully sing of life beyond the ghetto walls, even though hunger raged in their bellies and malnutrition and disease ravaged their small, frail bodies.[9]

Sheva could not save them then, but now she would breathe life back into these small ghosts that inhabited the shadows of her life. She would give them the greatest gift of all, immortality. In 1974, *Children of the Ghetto* was published in Yiddish under the patronage of Isaac Rubinstein, editor of the *Yiddishe Nayes*, the Yiddish supplement of the *Jewish News*.[10]

The story of the 1.5 million murdered children of the Holocaust, in this case the 1600 orphans of Marysin, whose short lives were so brutally extinguished, touched Mina deeply. Not just because Mina had a particular empathy for orphaned Jewish children, or that Holocaust survivors held a special place in her heart, nor was it merely an act of goodwill. Mina came to champion Sheva's Yiddish book because she was spurred on by a greater cause, an educational mission. Mina believed that stories such as this had the power to transform, to educate a new generation about the consequences of irrational hatred, brutal discrimination and unbridled violence, of government sanctioned racism that led to genocide.

The Task at Hand

Sheva was a member of the National Council of Jewish Women (NCJW) and Mina knew her well. At the book's launch, Mina spoke with conviction of her plans for the book's future. She knew that as the book was written in Yiddish, its readership would be limited. She made a pledge to have the text translated, republished and widely disseminated, to ensure that others understood and learnt from the lessons of the past.

> The Holocaust must take its rightful place in the education of the younger generation ... we must see to it that the message of the book, as a documentary, gets through to the maximum number of people. Let us put in some effort to see that the book is read in Yiddish, English, Hebrew, French, and Spanish. As a representative of the NCJW I will not spare myself and I will do all I can to promote the book and help Sheva Glas-Wiener to reach out to the younger age groups, who do not know Yiddish.[11]

Mina was an experienced community organiser and skilled networker. She knew what this commission entailed. 'The immediate task is to find the money and the audience', she told attendees at the Yiddish launch. She set out to do both. But it was a task that had many stops and starts as the NCJW prioritised projects and managed a range of ventures that called on limited resources. It also took Sheva time to undertake the translation and to work with a suitable translator. The English version had to remain true to the original text and not diminish the essence of its Yiddish soul. Mina demonstrated her own commitment to the project with a donation from the 'Leo and Mina Fink Fund'. Mina enlisted the NCJW in both Melbourne and Sydney to sponsor the book, raise money to have it translated and assist to underwrite the cost of its publication. She personally oversaw every stage of the process with dogged determination. Sheva's English version took nearly eight years to reach its new audience. Once the translation was ready for publication, Mina organised a committee that met regularly to plan how the book would be marketed and disseminated. Any profits would go towards NCJW projects in Israel. Mina was determined that the lives of the murdered children, children who were denied the right to grow old, had to count for a greater good.

Children of the Ghetto is Launched and Receives Unexpected Coverage

On Sunday 27 February 1983 at 5pm, the long-awaited English edition of *Children of the Ghetto* was launched at the Beth Weizmann Jewish Community Centre under the auspices of the NCJW. Mina, as convenor of the book launch committee, and her team of some 15 volunteers had overseen every detail of the launch, its publicity and the books ongoing sales. The book was officially launched by Dennis Pryor, reader of Classical Studies at the University of Melbourne and *The Age* newspaper columnist. 'That the children of the ghetto should have played "ghetto games" seems to me an obscenity unparalleled in the history of mankind', Pryor said. 'Sheva Glas-Wiener has honoured us by giving us the chance to read the stories of these children', he went on to say. 'She is part of all that recording, writing and remembering which must go on so that mankind may never forget what happened', he concluded. Both Isi Leibler, president of the Executive Council of Australian Jewry and Diane Alley, national president of NCJW spoke at the launch. Diane Alley spoke of the strength of the human spirit 'which rose above such a tremendous expression of man's inhumanity to man'. Isi Leibler spoke of its enduring message. 'To ensure that in the same way that the Exodus has been taught for 2000 years from generation to generation, the Holocaust will be conveyed to our children from generation to generation, both its nature and lessons that we learn today.'[12]

The book was published by Globe Press, a small local publisher in George Street, Fitzroy. Its cover had a photo of the children wearing their identifiable yellow star, being loaded onto the death train. The photographer is unknown but the photo is archived at Yad Vashem, Israel's Holocaust museum in Jerusalem. The same photo was used at a war crimes trial to convict Helmut Krizons, charged with atrocities committed in the ghetto in 1942. Sheva gave sworn evidence at a special hearing in Melbourne in May 1983 under an arrangement between the West German Government and the Australian Attorney General's Department. The involvement of Melbourne residents in the trial of a Nazi war criminal made it into the local press and Sheva was again interviewed. *Children of the Ghetto* received wide coverage as a result. At the hearing Sheva verified the photograph and identified Krizons as one of the SS officers who took part in the deportation of the children in September 1942.[13] He was convicted in West Germany in January 1985, but received a light sentence of only three years due to conflicting evidence and the charge of murder being dropped in place of the lesser charge of helping to deport at least 15,000 Lodz ghetto Jews. Krizons maintained that he was just following orders.

Spreading the Word

Mina was relentless in ensuring the book reached a wide audience. She lobbied the Sydney branch of the NCJW to relaunch the book later in the year. Author Thomas Keneally did the honours at the Sydney Jewish Book Fair in October 1983.[14] Copies of the book were sent to libraries here and overseas. Universities and schools were offered copies for their libraries in the hope that it would be incorporated in their teaching and in their curricular. Jewish, local and international newspapers were given complimentary copies to write reviews.[15] Many reviews subsequently appeared in the daily and international press. Sheva Glas-Wiener was interviewed by newspaper reporters, on radio and television. Of the 1000 print run, Mina personally sold 122 copies. The Victorian branch of NCJW sold nearly 200 copies. The International Council of Jewish Women were also sent copies to their branches overseas for wide dissemination. The Lodz *landsmanshaft* in Melbourne offered to promote the book and were active with sales through their own networks, as did other Holocaust survivor organisations both here and abroad. *Children of the Ghetto* was widely acknowledged as making an important contribution towards an understanding of the tragedy that was the Holocaust. Mina had completed this mission, but a far greater task lay ahead.

Testimonies, Telling the Truth about the Holocaust

The story of the Holocaust, as told by the eyewitnesses, heralded the start of a new era. For Mina and the survivors, eyewitness testimonies took on greater relevance and urgency as a new enemy emerged, an enemy that sought to discredit and delegitimise the Holocaust. Holocaust denial.

On 23 February 1983 Sheva told a reporter from *The Age* that she was sickened and frightened by so-called 'historians' claiming that the Holocaust never happened. 'We are getting old, the survivors. We are weak. In another 20 years there will be no one to tell the story. You have to do what you can to make sure it doesn't happen again … [that is why] I must tell the story.' 'I feel that writing about the Holocaust is a responsibility for those who survived', Sheva told a reporter for Sydney's *The Australian Jewish Times* on 27 October 1983. 'Young people have to know, so that it can never happen again.' 'We witnesses who are still alive have to answer those who say it never happened.'

Holocaust denial, a manifestation of post-war antisemitism, is almost as old as the Holocaust itself. What began in France in the late 1940s, was soon taken up by other antisemites and conspiracy theorists. Until the 1970s Holocaust denial was primarily the provenance of fringe extremists and racist groups. But then it seemed to gain traction, particularly in the United States and in Europe, quickly becoming a platform of the radical extreme right. Holocaust deniers hide their hateful antisemitic ideology under the guise of falsified historical scholarship. In an attempt to debunk the historical record, Holocaust deniers focused on four central pillars of the Holocaust: the number of Jewish victims, arguing that the murdered 6 million, a figure that was first validated at the International Military Tribunal at Nuremberg (which convened between 20 November 1945 and 1 October 1946), was a gross exaggeration; the gas chambers, claiming that they either did not exist or were not used for mass extermination; that there was no blueprint document for Hitler's Final Solution, bringing into doubt that mass extermination actions were ever sanctioned by the Third Reich; and finally, that Israel was either implicated in the Holocaust as a means of ensuring its creation, or that it directly came to profit from the Holocaust in the way of reparation payments from Germany. What the pre-eminent Holocaust historian Christopher Browning called 'this insidious movement ... [with] its pervasive contempt for the truth' and what Deborah Lipstadt proved, was that Holocaust denial was 'an assault on truth and memory'.[16]

For many survivors the travesty of denying the Holocaust was like a dagger piercing their hearts. It not only negated the horror of their lived experiences, but desecrated the memory of murdered family members, innocent men, women and children, whose only crime was their religion. While survivors had always borne witness to the Holocaust, an event without precedence, an event that challenged the very limits of language, many had confined their talk within closed circles, to fellow survivors, a community of fellow travellers, those who understood and accepted without judgement, without question the experiences they knew all too well. In the face of outrageous lies and unsubstantiated denial, their memories would now burst forth in a torrent of public truth telling. Many ageing survivors, now fearing their own mortality, were galvanised to step up and make public their very private experiences before it was too late.[17]

Holocaust survivors began emerging as a new force to combat those who challenged their past. More importantly they wanted to ensure that the future of Holocaust memory would not only document the past but would be instructive, that it would add pedagogical value. They would do so by providing evidence to an unprecedented dark page of history. They would substantiate the historical record with eyewitness testimony, personal, human stories that put flesh and blood onto the stark statistics and documents that bore the cold hard facts of mass murder. As Holocaust survivor and Nobel Peace Prize–winner

Eli Wiesel reminded his fellow survivors, 'to be a witness to an event such as the Holocaust is a burden but also a privilege'. This would be their assault on those who said it never happened.

The passage of time also brought with it a new audience, as a new generation emerged who were one step removed from the horrors that had engulfed the Jewish world and one step away from knowing and understanding what had happened. This audience was now ready and willing to engage with the survivors and their past, it was an audience that accepted 'memory' as a valid exploration of that past, its trauma as an important indicator of moral truths and as an arbitrator of social justice. This new audience valued the significance of victim narratives in documenting the past.[18]

Mina always had a canny understanding of the times in which she lived. She was adept at reading the mood of her community, the directions in which it moved and what it needed. Mina saw herself as having a pivotal role in bringing together those survivors now willing to speak and the audience now willing to listen and learn. This mission would be Mina's most enduring and final legacy.

Building a Holocaust Museum for the Future

In the beginning, Holocaust commemorations were all about heroism and resistance. Starting in 1944 on the first anniversary of the Warsaw ghetto uprising, the fight of the Jewish resistance against Nazi oppression became the ongoing symbol for major commemorative and communal Holocaust memorial services in Melbourne. In the ensuing decades the Warsaw ghetto revolt and all acts of resistance were the cornerstone of major Holocaust commemorations. As the number of Holocaust survivors in Melbourne swelled so did the number who attended these events, attracting thousands every year. In 1961 a Warsaw ghetto exhibition was mounted at the Melbourne Town Hall, attracting over 6000 non-Jewish visitors. The growing success of temporary exhibitions together with the broader appeal of community commemorations throughout the 1960s and '70s, gave impetus to the notion of a permanent museum to memorialise the Holocaust. The resounding success of the 1980 Holocaust exhibition in the Royal Exhibition Building in Carlton, with some 7500 attendees in addition to 2500 school students, demonstrated beyond doubt that it was time to mount a more permanent memorial. But this was now also the era of the living witness. It meant that the voices of the survivors would also have to be heard and incorporated into any permanent exhibition that commemorated the dead.[19]

In 1983 plans were already well advanced for a place where survivors in Melbourne could ensure their personal stories would be told as a cautionary tale, not just against the particular scourge of antisemitism, but also against the universal by targeting all forms of bigotry and racism.[20]

Although the impetus for a Holocaust museum came from within the survivor community and its permanent exhibition was designed and constructed by the survivors themselves, Mina's role should not be underestimated. Although Mina was not a survivor, her deep empathy and connection to the survivor community was profound. She saw herself as part of their world. It was what had propelled her into community service in the first place. She was determined to be a part of the development of Holocaust remembrance in Melbourne, the home to the largest Holocaust survivor community, per capita, outside of Israel. But for Mina it was essential to play the long game. She was convinced that the museum's greatest strength lay in its message, a message that should reverberate in perpetuity. Just as she had championed Sheva's book for its power to transform the reader, the museum's retelling of the Holocaust had to be an instructive lesson, an active educational tool for the living and for the future, and not just a passive, albeit important memorial to the dead and the past.

Mina became a vocal and active contributor to the museum's first organising committee which understandably focused on governance, construction and finance. She was valued for her attention to detail, her organisational skills and her ability to engage a large number of co-workers and volunteers. On 9 November 1983 Mina was elected president of the Appeal Committee for the Jewish Holocaust Centre (JHC), donating a personal gift of $50,000 towards the purchase of the two-storey building next to the Kadimah Hall in Selwyn Street, Elsternwick. This would be named 'Leo Fink House'.[21]

The official opening of the Jewish Holocaust Centre on 4 March 1984 attracted a huge crowd, estimated at 1500, who had to be seated outdoors in the carpark. Mina sat at the main head table. Above her hung a banner which proclaimed 'Remember the Six Million Jews'. Following Hershel Bachrach's dedication of the building in Leo Fink's name, Mina unveiled a plaque naming the museum building in honour of her late husband. This museum, one of the first of its kind in the world, was opened by Dr Itzhak Arad, director general of Yad Vashem in Jerusalem. The formal proceedings concluded with a rendition of the *Partisaner March (the Partisan's song)* composed by Hersh Glik in the Vilna ghetto in 1943.[22] Since the end of the Holocaust it was common practice for survivors to conclude commemorative events with what had become its battle hymn. On this occasion, not only was it a tribute to the heroism of the resistance fighters but served as a timely reminder that the fight, this time for the memory of the Holocaust, was just beginning.

On 6 March 1984 Mina was asked to form and lead a finance committee, focusing on the museum's financial viability and sustainability.
On 3 May she was confirmed as an 'advisor' to the JHC.[23] Mina took
her role seriously, offering advice and instruction on all organisational
matters, and became a major influence on the JHC's community fundraising. In its early days, she quickly became a public face of the centre.
Mina was a well-known community figure, a confident, accomplished
speaker, even though she always believed her English 'was not good
enough'. As patron of Adela Shaw's stained-glass memorial windows
on the first floor of the JHC's Leo Fink House, Mina gave the opening
address in English at their unveiling on 16 December 1984. When
Sheva Glas-Wiener died in 1986, Mina spoke at Sheva's *shloshim*
evening, traditionally held at the end of the 30-day mourning period,
at the JHC on 27 October.[24]

1985 Sets the Template: Education, 'Experts' and Outreach

By the end of 1985 the museum had made huge strides forward, setting
the template for its future operations. Mina's vision of the museum
as a dynamic, progressive institution had quickly taken shape. Mina
believed that organisations had to have the capacity to constantly
renew themselves in order to remain relevant to the community they
served, otherwise they would not survive. It had been the hallmark
of her leadership style for Jewish Welfare and the NCJW. You always
had to look to the future. For the JHC to remain relevant and to
address contemporary needs, Mina pushed for a forward-thinking,
quality education program, regular public lectures and the ongoing,
professional training of guides. This was the only way to sustain interest
in and engagement of audiences well into the future.

Throughout 1985 the JHC hosted 100 schools of various denominations, some coming from as far away as Korumburra and Rochester, bringing approximately 7000 students in all, as well as hundreds of overseas, interstate and local visitors, all of whom listened to survivor guides tell of their experiences and what lessons they thought could be learnt from the past. Today, approximately 23,000 students visit the JHC per year and benefit from its educational program, which remains the flagship of the centre.[25]

On 13 May 1985, the museum hosted a visit by Beate Klarsfeld, who, together with her husband Serge Klarsfeld, had made a name for herself as an activist and a fearless Nazi hunter. In August that year Professor Yehuda Bauer, renowned Holocaust scholar and academic at Hebrew University, Jerusalem, conducted a seminar and a public lecture. In October a temporary exhibition 'Art of the Holocaust' was launched with guest speakers Dulcie Kanatopsky, Adela Shaw and Paul Bartrop. Throughout 1985 a number of symposiums and lectures on the Holocaust were delivered by local academics, teacher seminars were held and a lecture was given by Dr Mark Verstandig on Jewish historians who died in the Holocaust. Public lectures remain a strong and important feature of the JHC's outreach to this day, as do invitations to leading public figures.[26]

It was important that the Jewish Holocaust Centre take its place amongst other public institutions as a museum and educational centre of repute. In 1985, the JHC became a member of the Melbourne Tourism Authority, hosted a visit by minister for the arts, Mr Race Mathews, and was awarded a grant from the Multicultural Institute for a project to combat racial prejudice. Most importantly the JHC was appointed by Yad Vashem as their official representative in Australia for collecting and compiling testimonies of survivors for their database. All of this was of critical importance to Mina. It meant recognition for the JHC and acknowledgement of its status.[27]

But it was in the education of the guides, all of whom were Holocaust survivors, and in the broader educational outreach that Mina really left her mark. Above all, Mina stressed the importance of professionalism. Mina liked to draw on 'experts', those whom she held in high esteem, those who had the educational credentials and experience to deliver instructive programs. Mina saw no place for amateurish activities. She was adamant that survivor guides undergo formal training, both to support the volunteers and to ensure that each visit was an effective educational experience. Academics Naomi Rosh White and Bernard Rechter joined Mina to form the 'guides group' and undertook the first training program. Mina arranged for experienced National Gallery of Victoria guides to come to the JHC to talk to survivor guides about the 'art' of guiding. Jenny Wajsenberg, a young dynamic educator, also set up projects, ran seminars for teachers and established links with Yad Vashem's teacher training program.[28]

Over the next three years Mina remained deeply involved with the centre, its survivor guides, its programs and its fundraising. She supported the inaugural curator Saba Feniger, herself a survivor of the Lodz ghetto and now a volunteer, to have ongoing professional development and to be given a dedicated space for her work. Saba recalled how Mina offered her encouragement and support, 'knowing that I had Mina's backing I was encouraged to go on and undertake a variety of commitments which I might otherwise not have been game enough to do'.[29] Mina lobbied the JHC to forge broader educational links by subscribing to international journals and regularly inviting visiting scholars.

In 1986 she supported the centre's plans for expansion as long as the educational focus remained at the forefront. It did then, as it does now.

In June 1988 Mina resigned from the executive of the JHC, allegedly in protest over the organisation and running of its meetings.[30] It was a spat over process not ideology. Mina remained a stickler for correct record keeping and orderly procedures and did not tolerate disorganised meetings. She nevertheless remained a staunch supporter of the JHC for the rest of her life. Her personal relationship with the survivor guides remained strong and her commitment to the work of the executive was unwavering. The future of the JHC was assured.

Beyond the Institutions

While Mina's work with organisations took up a large part of her life, her impact went far beyond the institutional level, often reaching out to individuals and championing personal causes that struck an emotional chord within her. 'She always saw beyond the institution – every person she encountered was an individual who mattered', her granddaughter Lillian Tell recalled.[31]

In a letter to the president of the Melbourne Jewish Philanthropic Society on 3 March 1986, Mina successfully asked for special consideration and immediate admission to the Montefiore Homes for the Aged, of former Yiddish actress and welfare worker Rachel Holzer, who was living in extreme hardship in a non-Jewish institution: 'She devoted her whole life to the strengthening of Jewish culture ... her contribution to ... our community is indeed difficult to measure ... the community for whom she worked and to whom she gave so much is entitled to ensure that Rachel Holzer is able to enter the Montefiore Homes immediately'. Rachel Holzer lived the last years of her life in Jewish aged care.[32]

Her work with individuals went beyond the living. When passing an unmarked, unkept grave of a person unknown to her at Springvale Jewish cemetery, Mina was outraged that a human being could just sink into the earth, without leaving any mark of a life once lived. Such tragedies happened in the Holocaust. But here? Now? She successfully lobbied the authorities for the grave to be given a tombstone.[33] Every individual needed to be remembered. It was a sacred Jewish obligation.

On 11 February 1985, Mina accepted an invitation to be a key sponsor of the 'Free Wallenberg' committee, spearheaded by Wallenberg survivor Dr Frank Vajda.[34] Raoul Wallenberg was a Swedish businessman and diplomat who is remembered for his heroic efforts in saving nearly 10,000 Hungarian Jews while assigned to the Swedish Legation in Budapest from July until October 1944. Wallenberg was arrested by the Soviets on 16 January 1945 on disputed charges of espionage. His fate remains a mystery, though current understanding is that he died while in Soviet captivity. On 26 November 1963, Yad Vashem recognised Raoul Wallenberg as 'Righteous Among the Nations', a title bestowed on non-Jews who took great risks to save Jews during the Holocaust. Rescue took many forms and the 'Righteous' came from different nations, religions and walks of life. What they had in common was that they showed great moral courage in protecting Jews at a time when most did not.

Resilient and Steadfast until the End

In the face of her own personal tragedies and difficulties, Mina remained resilient and forward thinking. Her early life as an orphan raised by grandparents, leaving behind the turbulent, culturally rich world of Bialystok after her fortuitous marriage to Leo, the tragic impact of the Holocaust, the death of Leo and both her brothers within two years of each other, all of which never deterred her from the tasks she set herself. But there was one tragedy that came late in her life. One tragedy that nearly broke her.

The sudden and tragic death of Mina's grandchild, Naomi Segev (Fink), on 21 December 1988 devastated her. It was a tragedy from which she never fully recovered. While Mina enjoyed a warm and loving relationship with all her six grandchildren, she had been particularly close to Naomi, her youngest grandchild. Mina never outwardly complained or indulged in self-pity. She remained stoic. Although left with an ache in her heart, she did not publicly grieve; her concern was always for the welfare of others.[35]

And so it was in her own last days. In April 1990 Mina suffered a heart attack. While recovering in a hospital's cardiac ward, she showed little concern for her own welfare, preferring to offer lifestyle advice to three other patients in the ward, 'all healthier than her as it happened', her son Nathan recalled.[36] On 2 May 1990, following a period of recovery, Mina died suddenly and unexpectedly of a cardiac arrest. She was buried in the Chevra Kadisha cemetery in Springvale, the same cemetery that had housed the unmarked grave for which she fought so hard to have a tombstone erected.

Mina's life of service, shared with Leo and later without him, started with the Holocaust and fittingly ended with it. What had catapulted Mina into social action began with the greatest existential threat to the Jewish world, and ended with the battle for its memory. The journey in between was a quest for the continuity of Jewish life and the preservation of Jewish humanity. In all this she was relentless. Survival of the Jewish world was what sustained her, as it had Leo. She was part of that world and that world was part of her. Indivisible.

LEGACY

The life that Leo and Mina chose to live was driven by their abiding commitment to the Jewish world, its survival and its continuity. That was first brought into stark relief during the Holocaust. As Leo recalled shortly before his death in 1972: 'The Holocaust shattered me. I felt that we cannot accept the situation with resignation. Something had to be done'. For Leo this meant action, not just rhetoric. In 1944 he spelt out the task that lay ahead:

> We must continue to develop the work in every possible direction and be prepared for the many tasks that await us. When the guns cease firing ... when the war will finally come to its victorious conclusion – and we know that this day is not far off – the Jewish battle for bringing our brethren back to health and normal life will just begin. When Europe is finally freed, the remnants of European Jewry will present a ghastly picture of havoc and utter misery. They can be helped only by a concerted and sustained effort of their fellow Jews in the free countries. In this global effort of world Jewry, we Jews in Australia will have to play a part that far outweighs our numerical strength.[1]

For Mina, the Holocaust was deeply personal. 'When we worked for the Relief Fund, we worked for ourselves. There wasn't one of us who hadn't lost someone in the war ... It was our aim to help rebuild lives ...'[2] Mina's devotion to her 'Buchenwald Boys' spanned decades and only ended with her death in 1990.

The Holocaust also instilled in Mina a strong sense of purpose, an enduring commitment to those less fortunate. In an interview with the *Australian Jewish News* on 11 September 1987, she revealed how this came to be. 'I have a deep feeling for underprivileged people. After the War, the shock of what had happened touched me greatly. I put all my personal efforts into relief fund work. Community service has become my life's work.'

Leo and Mina's belief in self-help and self-reliance stemmed from their experiences growing up in Bialystok. As Leo reflected in a speech written shortly before his death and quoted at his *shloshim* on 23rd October 1972:

> I was born in the Shtetl and regard myself as a Shtetl product: a Jew who brought with him qualifications bred in the life of the Shtetl, which is a combination of many factors; its stark realism and its sensitive romanticism; a rational appreciation of human values as well as an understanding of their failings in the struggle for survival against great odds; a love for humanity and for one's fellow man.[3]

This trait, this tradition of communal service was recognised by others. In a letter of condolence written to Mina on Leo's death in September 1972, Alec Masel recalled, 'He was, as are you [Mina], steeped in the Bialystoker tradition of service to our less fortunate brothers and sisters and our community is greatly indebted to him for his long-standing leadership in good causes'. In a powerful eulogy for Mina Fink delivered on 4 May 1990, community stalwart Walter Lippmann linked Mina's connection to the Jewish world to her early life in Bialystok. 'Brought up in the kehillah of Bialystok, Mina had an abiding commitment to the Jewish people and her concern for the welfare of our people led her to a lifetime involvement with communal organisations.'[4]

Leo and Mina were both visionaries, always with an eye for the big picture. In the post-war era, both could see the benefit of bringing Holocaust survivors to Australia, not just for their own rehabilitation but for the benefit of the local community, small in size and therefore vulnerable. 'On today's immigration depends the survival of Jewish communal life in this country', Leo proclaimed in 1947. 'We can replenish and revitalise our stock today. Tomorrow it may be too late.' Shortly before his death Leo reiterated the benefit of bringing survivors to these distant shores. 'We had a philosophy of recreating a Jewish group life in a vibrant, cohesive Jewish community here in Australia.' Rabbi Schreiber of the Kew Hebrew congregation spoke of Leo's vision at his funeral. 'It was his historic privilege to become and to remain a Jewish pioneer who used the best of yesterday for the upbuilding of the Jewish tomorrow.'[5]

Leo and Mina had a strong belief that charity had to be uplifting, enabling and a means of rehabilitating individuals so that they would become self-sufficient. This was noted in Leo's obituary in the *Australian Jewish News* on 29 September, 1972. 'He was unique in his generation – an industrialist and an intellectual who believed that the unfortunate of the world were entitled not to charity but to the means for their own rehabilitation.' Leo and Mina's son, Nathan Fink, spoke of this quality at his own son's bar mitzvah in 1975. 'He [Leo] saw the true purpose of his welfare work to be the uplifting of the migrant and the underprivileged so that they, in turn, could not only receive but in future would be the best people to help others.'[6] Lillian Tell, Mina and Leo's granddaughter spoke of Mina's belief in the power of the individual to overcome adversity. 'Mina Fink believed in the ability of the individual to change things.'[7]

Late in her life Mina understood the need to expand community services to embrace a raft of additional pressing needs. In an article for the *Australian Jewish News* on 4 September 1987 she explained, 'We have a sacred obligation to maintain and if necessary, extend the services for the aged, for the young, for the physically and mentally handicapped'.

Mina Fink enthusiastically embraced the feminist cause. She saw the push for equality as a means of pursuing natural justice. Women had to be equals, they had to lead and they had to encourage others to do so. 'Men were inclined to think that women were there to "make the tea", and really I don't see why they shouldn't make the tea for us, sometimes', Mina told a journalist for the *Courier Mail* on 16 June 1970. 'We are almost there in this equality battle. What we need now, to bridge the gap, is the help of the men, and the women must seek this help,' she concluded. 'Mina Fink was a feminist in the best sense of the word', remarked Sylvia Gelman at a commemorative evening honouring Mina Fink on 17 June 1990. Gelman credited Mina with inspiring others to lead. 'It is a reflection of her concern for women to assume active and leadership roles in the life of the community that I and many others were inspired by her to become involved and assume positions in NCJW and other organisations.'

Mina's work ethic and her belief in education as the pathway to ensure a better world was reflected in her work in establishing the Holocaust museum in Melbourne. In a report written in 1990, the museum remembered Mina's service and her dedication to its educational mission. 'Mina was indefatigable, involved in setting up the Holocaust Centre's administrative structure and serving on the Board. Her particular interest was the educational program and the training of Holocaust survivors as guides.'

Together, Leo and Mina were an inspirational, devoted team. They worked hand in glove. After Leo's passing, Mina continued the work, her principled commitment to communal service paramount. The memory of Leo remained a constant presence in her life, his influence undiminished over the years. At a memorial service for Mina in 1990, Johnny Baker, the son of one of Mina's beloved Buchenwald Boys recalled the strength of their partnership. 'It is impossible to speak of Mina without uniting her with her late husband Leo Fink. Although he passed away many years before her, she spoke of him to the last, always as a constant companion and a source of guidance. They worked together as a team and they complimented one another in their varied activities.'

Their work continues to this day; their legacy endures. Leo and Mina's grandchildren have taken up the baton passed to them by their grandparents. Eldest granddaughter Deborah Golvan explained, 'We feel it is our duty to carry on our grandparents' project ... they taught us the value of volunteering and philanthropy ... giving time and money to organisations that are doing important work has provided us with a sense of purpose and community involvement. Hopefully, these things are making the world a better place'. Grandson Alex Freiberg added, 'Volunteering time and funds is a way to balance the moral compass'. For Leo and Mina Fink taught them the greatest lesson of all: ensure that what you do is always for the greater good.

NOTES

Chapter 1: Against the Odds

1 *Sydney Jewish News*, 21 March 1947.
2 *Daily Telegraph*, 17 March 1947.
3 *Sydney Morning Herald*, 17 March 1947; *Daily Telegraph*, 17 March 1947.
4 *Barrier Miner*, 18 March 1947.
5 *Barrier Miner*, 18 March 1947.
6 *Daily Telegraph*, 17 March 1947.
7 *Newcastle Morning Herald*, 17 March 1947.
8 *Singleton Argus*, 17 March 1947.
9 *Barrier Miner*, 18 March 1947.
10 *Sydney Jewish News*, 21 March 1947.
11 Margaret Taft and Andrew Markus, *A Second Chance, The Making of Yiddish Melbourne* (Melbourne: Monash University Publishing, 2018), 157.
12 *Melbourne Herald*, 31 January 1947.
13 Taft and Markus, *A Second Chance, The Making of Yiddish Melbourne*, 154.
14 Suzanne Rutland, '"I Never Knew A Man Who Had So Many Cousins": Differing Attitudes to Postwar Survivor Migration: Melbourne and Sydney', *Australian Jewish Historical Society Journal* XII, Part 2 (1994).
15 'Leo Fink – A Tribute', *Centre News*, June 1987.
16 UJORF Executive Board minutes, 26 February 1946.
17 James Jupp, cited in John Huxley, 'When the Boat Came In', *The Age*, 2007. https://www.theage.com.au/national/when-the-boat-came-in-20070311-ge4e9h.html.
18 Taft and Markus, *A Second Chance, The Making of Yiddish Melbourne*, 158.
19 Letter to Fink from Arthur Calwell (Fink Papers Melbourne University, Box 2/Folder 2).
20 Letter to Fink from Arthur Calwell (Fink Papers Melbourne University, Box 2/Folder 2).
21 Letter to Fink from Saul Symonds (Fink Papers Melbourne University, Box 1/Folder 11).
22 Fink Family private papers.
23 *The Australian Jewish News*, 11 September 1987, 23.
24 *Daily Telegraph*, 11 February 1947, 5.
25 *Welcare*, September 1987.
26 *Daily Telegraph*, 11 February 1947, 5.
27 *Daily Telegraph*, 11 February 1947, 5.

28   *Daily Telegraph*, 17 March 1947.

29   Klaus Neumann, *Across the Seas: Australia's Response to Refugees, a History* (Melbourne: Black Inc., 2015), 94.

30   O.A. Oeser and S.B. Hammond, *Social Structure and Personality in a City* (London: Routledge, 1954).

31   Taft and Markus, *A Second Chance, The Making of Yiddish Melbourne*, 154–58.

32   Alexandra Fanny Brodsky, *In Pursuit of a Dream; A Time in Australia* (London & NY: The Radcliffe Press, 2007), 75–78.

33   *Daily Telegraph*, 17 March 1947.

34   Peter Plowman, *Australian Migrant Ships 1946–77* (Sydney: Rosenberg Publishing, 2006).

35   *Welcare*, September 1987.

36   *Sun*, 18 March 1947; *Sydney Jewish News*, 25 April 1947.

Chapter 2: There's Something about Bialystok

1   Fink Family private papers.

2   Rebecca Kobrin, *Jewish Bialystok and Its Diaspora* (Bloomington: Indiana University Press, 2010), 14.

3   'Białystok', The YIVO Encyclopedia of Jews in Eastern Europe, 2010, https://yivoencyclopedia.org/article.aspx/Bialystok.

4   Kobrin, *Jewish Bialystok and Its Diaspora*, 6.

5   Fink Family private papers.

6   Fink Family private papers.

7   Original document held in Fink Family private papers.

8   David E. Fishman, *The Rise of Modern Yiddish Culture* (Pittsburgh: University of Pittsburgh Press, 2005), 83–137.

9   David, Sohn, ed., *Byalistok bilder album fun a barimter shtot un yire yiden yiber der welt, [Białystok Photo Album of a Renowned City and its Jews the World Over.]* (New York: Bialystoker Center, 1951).

10 Kobrin, *Jewish Bialystok and Its Diaspora*, 9.

11 David, Sohn, ed., *Byalistok bilder album fun a barimter shtot un yire yiden yiber der welt, [Białystok Photo Album of a Renowned City and its Jews the World Over.]*

12 Kobrin, *Jewish Bialystok and Its Diaspora*, 14.

13 'Białystok'.

14 Walter Laqueur, *History of Zionism* (New York: Schocken Books, 1989).

15 Bernard Wasserstein, *On the Eve: The Jews of Europe Before the Second World War* (New York: Simon & Schuster, 2012), 68–72.

16 'Zamenhof, Ludwik', The YIVO Encyclopedia of Jews in Eastern Europe, 2010, https://yivoencyclopedia.org/article.aspx/Zamenhof_Ludwik.

17 Yaacov Ro'l, ed., *Jews and Jewish life in Russia and the Soviet Union* (Essex: Frank Cass & Co. Ltd., 1995), 135–7.

18 Edward Madigan & Gideon Reuveni, eds. *The Jewish Experience of the First World War* (London: Palgrave Macmillan), 2019.

19 'Białystok'.

20 Kobrin, *Jewish Bialystok and Its Diaspora*, 69.

21 Nathan Fink, *Talking Histories: Mina Fink*, 11 December 2002.

22 Original document held in Fink Family private papers.

23 Götz Aly, *Europe Against the Jews, 1880–1945* (New York: Metropolitan Books, 2020), 104–134.

24 'Russian Civil War', The YIVO Encyclopedia of Jews in Eastern Europe, 2010, https://yivoencyclopedia.org/article.aspx/Russian_Civil_War.

25 Freda Freiberg, interview by Margaret Taft (South Yarra, Victoria, 13 December 2018).

26 Freiberg, Interview.

27 Miriam Eisenstein, *Jewish Schools in Poland 1919–39: Their Philosophy and Development* (New York: Columbia Press, 1950).

28 Original school certificate in Fink Family private papers.

29 Paula Hyman, 'Eastern European Jewish Women in an Age of Transition, 1880–1930', in *Jewish Women in Historical Perspective*, ed. Judith Baskin (Detroit: Wayne State University Press, 1998), 216–21; ChaeRan Freeze, Paula Hyman, and Antony Polonsky, eds. *Polin: Studies in Polish Jewry Volume 18: Jewish Women in Eastern Europe* (Portland, OR: The Littman Library of Jewish Civilization, 2007).

30 Original school certificate in Fink Family private papers.

Chapter 3: Becoming Leo

1 Freda Freiberg, interview by Margaret Taft (South Yarra, Victoria, 13 December 2018).

2 Jonathan Schneer, *The Balfour Declaration* (London: Bloomsbury Publishing, 2010).

3 Yehoshua Ben-Arieh, *The Making of Eretz Israel in the Modern Era* (Jerusalem: Hebrew University Magnes Press, 2018), 422–27.

4 Mina Fink personal correspondence, 28 November 1986, Fink Family private papers.

5 'Rosh Pina', Jewish Virtual Library, https://www.jewishvirtuallibrary.org/rosh-pina.

6 'Palestine Census (1922)', Internet Archive, 2015, https://archive.org/details/PalestineCensus1922.

7 Henry Near, *The Kibbutz Movement: A History, Origins and Growth 1909–1939*, Vol. 1 (Oxford: Oxford University Press, 1992).

8   Fink Family private papers.
9   Tamar Wolf-Monzon, 'Uri Zvi Greenberg and the pioneers of the Third Aliyah: A Case of Reception', *Prooftexts* 29, no. 1 (2009).
10 Martin Gilbert, *Israel A History* (London: Doubleday, 1998), 36–59.
11 Freiberg, Interview.
12 Adam Sacks, 'Ostbahnhof Berlin', *Polin Studies* 32 (2020): 321–42.
13 Klaus Mann, *The Turning point: Thirty-five Years in this Century, the Autobiography of Klaus Mann* (Lexington: Plunkett Lake Press, 2017, c.1942).
14 'Josephine Baker: Goin' Bananas', Cabaret Berlin, 2010, https://cabaret.berlin/people/josephine-baker/.
15 Eric D. Weitz, 'Weimar Germany and its Histories', *Central European Histories* 43, no. 4 (2010): 581–591; 'The Weimar Republic', Holocaust Encyclopedia, https://encyclopedia.ushmm.org/content/en/article/the-weimar-republic.
16 Letter held in Fink Family private papers.

Chapter 4: New Beginnings

1   Keith Hitchins, *Rumania, 1866–1947* (Oxford: Oxford University Press, 1994).
2   Ibid.
3   'Galati', Jewish Virtual Library, 2008, https://www.jewishvirtuallibrary.org/galati. 'Galaţi', The YIVO Encyclopedia of Jews in Eastern Europe, 2010, https://yivoencyclopedia.org/article.aspx/Galati. Sadetsky-Kimron, Ayana, 'Galaţi, Romania', JewishGen KehilaLinks, 2008, https://kehilalinks.jewishgen.org/galati/galatz_history.htm.
4   Freiberg, Interview.
5   Original document held in Fink Family private papers.
6   . 'Citta di Genova', Passengers in History, https://passengers.history.sa.gov.au/node/922955.
7   Freiberg, Interview.
8   Taft and Markus, *A Second Chance: The Making of Yiddish Melbourne*, 6–7.
9   Charles A Price, 'Jewish Settlers in Australia', *Australian Jewish Historical Society Journal and Proceedings* V, Part 8 (1964): 375.
10 Taft and Markus, *A Second Chance: The Making of Yiddish Melbourne*, 29.
11 Geoffrey Blainey, *A History of Victoria* (Melbourne: Cambridge University Press, 2013), 181.
12 Newman Rosenthal, 'Immigrants on the Land', *Australian Jewish Herald*, 1 December 1927, 4.
13 'Jews as Farmers: Solving Australian Jewish Immigration Problem', *Hebrew Standard of Australasia*, 24 August 1928, 6; 'Destitute Jews', *The Age*, 22 February 1928.

14   Suzanne D Rutland, *Edge of the Diaspora: Two Centuries of Jewish Settlement in Australia* (Sydney: Brandl & Schlesinger Pty Ltd, 1997), 91.

15   Pam MacLean, 'Jewish Migration in the Twenties: A Jewish Pioneering Tradition in Australia?', *Meanjin* 42, no. 1 (March 1983): 47–54.

16   Barry Fink and Leon Fink, interview by Margaret Taft (Toorak, Victoria, 23 February 2019).

17   Freiberg, Interview.

18   Credit note in Fink Family private papers.

19   Blainey, *A History of Victoria*, 189–91.

20   Nathan Fink, interview by Margaret Taft (East Melbourne, Victoria, 27 November 2018).

21   Dorothy Rogers, *A History of Kew* (Melbourne: Lowden Publishing Company, 1973).

22   Colin Golvan, *The Distant Exodus* (Crows Nest, NSW: ABC Enterprises, 1990), 61.

23   Taft and Markus, *A Second Chance: The Making of Yiddish Melbourne*, 15.

Chapter 5: On the Brink

1   Freiberg, Interview.

2   Martin Gilbert, *Routledge Atlas of the Holocaust* (London: Routledge, 2002), 21.

3   Leo Cooper, *In the Shadow of the Polish Eagle: The Poles, the Holocaust and Beyond* (London: Palgrave Macmillan, 2000), 60.

4   Celia S Heller, *On the Edge of Destruction: Jews of Poland Between the Two World Wars* (Detroit: Wayne University Press, 1977), 77–114.

5   Ibid.

6   Heller, *On the Edge of Destruction: Jews of Poland Between the Two World Wars*, 107.

7   Taft and Markus, *A Second Chance*, 95.

8   Golvan, *The Distant Exodus*, 11.

9   Hilary Rubinstein, *The Jews in Australia, A Thematic History, Volume 1, 1788–1945* (Melbourne: William Heinemann Australia, 1991), 43.

10   Moshe Ajzenbud, *60 Years of 'Bund' in Melbourne 1928–1988* (Melbourne: Jewish Labour Bund, 1996).

11   Rodney Benjamin, *'A Serious Influx of Jews' A History of Jewish Welfare in Victoria* (St Leonards, NSW: Allen & Unwin, 1998), 64–7; Taft and Markus, *A Second Chance*, 100–1.

12   Kate Darian-Smith, *On the Home Front; Melbourne in Wartime: 1939–1945* (Melbourne: Melbourne University Press, 2009 (1990)), 2.

13   Darian-Smith, *On the Home Front; Melbourne in Wartime: 1939–1945*, 2–4.

14 'Black Friday Bushfires, 1939', Australian Disaster Resilience Knowledge Hub, https://knowledge.aidr.org.au/resources/bushfire-black-friday-victoria-1939/.
15 'Prime Minister Robert G. Menzies: wartime broadcast', Australian War Memorial, https://www.awm.gov.au/articles/encyclopedia/prime_ministers/menzies.

Chapter 6: 'A Matter of Life and Death'

1   Christopher Browning, *The Path to Genocide: Essays on Launching the Final Solution* (Cambridge: Cambridge University Press, 1992), 86–121.
2   Kadimah Annual Report, 1942.
3   Golvan, *The Distant Exodus*, 87.
4   Great Synagogue minutes 3 August 1939, cited in Rutland, *Edge of the Diaspora*, 202.
5   *Australian Jewish News*, 1 October 1976, 2.
6   Michael McKernan, *All In! Australia During the Second World War* (Melbourne: Thomas Nelson Australia, 1983), 26–7.
7   Darian-Smith, *On the Home Front*, 4.
8   Darian-Smith, *On the Home Front*, 4.
9   Fink Family private papers.
10 Darian-Smith, *On the Home Front*, 5.
11 Radio address, 30 August 1939, cited in Mark Dapin, *Jewish Anzacs: Jews in the Australian Military* (Sydney: New South Publishing, 2017), 159.
12 *Australian Jewish News*, 7 September 1939.
13 *Australian Jewish News*, 6 June 1940.
14 *Australian Jewish News*, 6 June 1940.
15 Walter Jona, 'The VAJEX Story: Achievements in War and Peace', *Australian Jewish Historical Society Journal* XII, no. 1 (1993): 171–8.
16 Original documents in Fink Family private papers.
17 Joan Beaumont, ed. *Australia's War, 1939–45* (Crows Nest: Allen & Unwin: 1996), 61–2.
18 Original documents in Fink Family private papers.
19 *Australian Jewish Herald*, 10 December 1942.
20 *Australian Jewish News*, 1 October 1976.
21 Kadimah Annual Report, 1942.
22 Benjamin, *A Serious Influx of Jews*, 142.
23 Cited in Benjamin, *A Serious Influx of Jews*, 143.
24 JPRF Board of Management minutes, 20 June 1943.
25 JPRF Executive meeting minutes, 7 July 1943.
26 UJRF Executive meeting minutes, 27 July 1943.
27 UJRF Board of Management meeting minutes, 26 September 1943.

28 UJRF Executive meeting minutes, 7 October 1943.
29 Kadimah Annual Report, 1943.
30 UJORF Board meeting minutes, 22 February 1944.
31 UJORF Executive meeting minutes, 15 January 1945.
32 *Australian Jewish Herald*, 26 January 1946.
33 *Australian Jewish News*, 8 December 1944.
34 *Australian Jewish News*, 13 April 1945.
35 UJORF Board meeting minutes, 15 May 1945.
36 Fink Family private papers.
37 UJORF Annual General Meeting report, 30 June 1944.
38 UJORF Annual General Meeting report, 30 June 1945.
39 Victory Year 1945: The Story of Melbourne Jewry's Contribution to Overseas Relief, UJORF June 1945.
40 UJORF Board meeting minutes, 18 September 1945.
41 Victory Year 1945: The Story of Melbourne Jewry's Contribution to Overseas Relief, UJORF June 1945.

Chapter 7: 'A Welcome, a Job, a Home and a Future'

1   Max Zilberman, *Talking Histories*, 11 December 2002.
2   Zilberman, *Talking Histories*.
3   'MS Eridan 1928–1956', Derby Sulzers, 2011, https://www.derbysulzers.com/shiperidan.html.
4   *Morning Bulletin*, 20 January 1949, 4.
5   Fink Family private papers.
6   Zilberman, *Talking Histories*.
7   Suzanne Rutland, 'Post war Anti-Jewish Refugee Hysteria: A case of Racial or Religious bigotry?' *Journal of Australian Studies* 27, no. 77 (2003).
8   Zilberman, *Talking Histories*.
9   *Australian Jewish Herald*, 21 November 1947.
10 *Australian Jewish News*, 11 September 1987.
11 Australian Jewish Welfare and Relief Society report 1953.
12 UJORF Board meeting minutes, 2 December 1947.
13 Rutland, *Edge of the Diaspora*, 241.
14 Zilberman, *Talking Histories*.
15 Rutland, *Edge of the Diaspora*, 241.
16 Benjamin, *A Serious Influx of Jews*, 5.
17 UJORF Executive Board meeting minutes, 8 July 1946.
18 AJWS Directors meeting minutes, 5 August 1946.
19 UJORF Board meeting minutes, 20 July 1948.
20 'A Record of the Activities of the Australian Jewish Welfare and Relief Society from 1943–1953', held in Fink Family private papers.

21 Letter held in Fink Family private papers.
22 AJWRS Annual Report 1947–48.
23 Cited in Golvan, *The Distant Exodus*, 87.
24 Fink letter to Brand, 11 July 1949.
25 Suzanne Rutland and Sol Encel, 'Three Rich Uncles in America', *American Jewish History* 95, no. 1 (2009).
26 Suzanne Rutland, 'Resettling Survivors of the Holocaust in Australia', *Holocaust Studies: A Journal of Culture and History* 16, no. 3 (2010).
27 Minutes of meeting between AJWRS Executive and Emery Komlos, 8 September 1949.
28 Ibid.
29 Emery Komlos, 'Survey of Jewish Migration and Settlement in Australia', 26 October 1949, file 438, France IV, HIAS-HICEM-NY.
30 Tony Dingle and Seamus O'Hanlon, 'Modernism versus domesticity: The contest to shape Melbourne's homes, 1945–1969', *Australian Historical Studies* 27 (1997).
31 Golvan, *The Distant Exodus*, 87.
32 Zilberman, *Talking Histories*.
33 Seamus O'Hanlon, 'Hostels for Migrant Workers in Early Postwar Melbourne', *History Australia* 2, no. 3 (2005).
34 Rutland, 'Resettling the Survivors of the Holocaust', 48.
35 *Australian Jewish News*, 11 September 1987.
36 AJWRS Board meeting minutes, 1 November 1948.
37 Fink Papers, Melbourne University Archive, 1990.0091.
38 *Australian Jewish News*, 11 September 1987.
39 'A Record of the Activities of the Australian Jewish Welfare and Relief Society from 1943–1953', held in Fink Family private papers.
40 Zilberman, *Talking Histories*.
41 Zilberman, *Talking Histories*.
42 *Australian Jewish News*, 11 September 1987.
43 'Leo Fink – A Tribute', *Centre News*, June 1987.
44 *Australian Jewish News*, 11 September 1987.
45 Fink Family private papers.
46 Fink Family private papers.

Chapter 8: 'The Lucky Fifties'

1 John Murphy, *Imagining the Fifties* (Sydney: UNSW Press, 2000), 13.
2 Peter Fitzpatrick, *After 'the Doll': Australian Drama Since 1955* (Melbourne: Edward Arnold (Australia), 1979).
3 'In competition – feature films JEDDA', Festival De Cannes World, 1955, http://www.festival-cannes.com/en/archives/ficheFilm/id/3702/year/1955.html.

4   Arnold Zable, *Wanderers and Dreamers: Tales of the David Herman Theatre* (Melbourne: Hyland Press, 1998).

5   Serge Liberman, 'Seventy Years of Yiddish Theatre in Melbourne (1909–1979)', Part 2, *Melbourne Chronicle*, January 1981.

6   Blundell, Graeme, 'Barry Humphries, the clown prince of suburbia', *The Australian*, 7 February 2009.

7   'John Michael O'Keefe 1935–1978', Australian Dictionary of Biography, 2000, http://adb.anu.edu.au/biography/okeefe-john-michael-johnny-11293.

8   'On the Beach', *Variety*, 1958, https://variety.com/1958/film/reviews/on-the-beach-1200419354/.

9   Peter Pierce, *The Cambridge History of Australian Literature* (Melbourne: Cambridge University Press, 2011).

10   'Judah Leon Waten 1911–1985', Australian Dictionary of Biography, 2012, http://adb.anu.edu.au/biography/waten-judah-leon-14884.

11   WD Rubinstein, *The Jews in Australia: A Thematic History, Volume 2: 1945 to the Present* (Melbourne: William Heinemann Australia, 1991), 334.

12   Fink Family private papers.

13   Taft and Markus, *A Second Chance*, 223–34.

14   Taft and Markus, *A Second Chance*, 235–42.

15   Fiona Allon, 'At home in the Suburbs', *History Australia* 11, no. 1 (2014).

16   Taft and Markus, *A Second Chance*, 189.

17   Judith Brett, *Robert Menzies' Forgotten People* (Carlton: Melbourne University Press, 2007); Nick Cater, 'Robert Menzies' Forgotten People', *The Australian*, 22 May 2012.

18   Fink Family private papers.

19   AJWRS Annual General Meeting report, 1950.

20   AJWRS Board meeting minutes.

21   AJWRS Board meeting minutes.

22   AJWRS Board meeting minutes.

23   Fink papers, Melbourne University Archives, 1990.0091.

24   AJWRS annual general meeting report, 1953.

25   Fink Family private papers.

26   Nick Richardson, *1956: The Year Australia Welcomed the World* (Melbourne: Scribe Publications, 2019).

27   AJWRS Annual General Meeting report, 1956.

28   AJWRS Annual General Meeting report, 1956.

29   Marlo Newton, *Making A Difference: A History of the National Council of Jewish Women* (Melbourne: Hybrid Publishers, 2000), 7–17.

30   NCJW Bulletin, June/July 1957.

31   NCJW Bulletin August/September 1957.

32   NCJW Bulletin April/May 1958.

33 NCJW Bulletin August/September 1958.
34 Benjamin, 'A Serious Influx of Jews', 266.
35 AJWRS Board meeting minutes, 12 February 1958.
36 AJWRS Annual Report, June 1959.

Chapter 9: A Pioneer Once More

1   Fink Family private papers.
2   Fink Family private papers.
3   Howard Sachar, *A History of Israel: From the Rise of Zionism to Our Times* (New York: Alfred A Knopf, 1996 (1979)).
4   'Israel's International Relations: Cooperation with Africa', Jewish Virtual Library, 2021, https://www.jewishvirtuallibrary.org/israeli-cooperation-with-africa.
5   'The Charge of the 4th Light Horse Brigade at Beersheba', Australian War Memorial, 2007, https://www.awm.gov.au/articles/blog/the-charge-of-the-4th-light-horse-brigade-at-beersheba.
6   'Sir John Monash 1865–1931', Australian Dictionary of Biography, 1986, http://adb.anu.edu.au/biography/monash-sir-john-7618.
7   Daniel Mandel, 'A Good International Citizen: H.V. Evatt, Britain, the United Nations and Israel, 1948–49', *Middle Eastern Studies* 39, no. 2 (April 2003): 82–104.
8   Colin Rubinstein and Tzvi Fleischer, 'A distant affinity: The History of Australian-Israeli Relations', *Jewish Political Studies Review* 19, no. 3/4 (Fall 2007): 101–124.
9   'Israeli Population Statistics (1960–2008)', Jewish Virtual Library, 2008, https://www.jewishvirtuallibrary.org/israeli-population-statistics-1960-2008.
10 'Fact Sheet: Jewish Refugees from Arab Countries', Jewish Virtual Library, https://www.jewishvirtuallibrary.org/jewish-refugees-from-arab-countries.
11 Fink Family private papers.
12 'Menachem Begin on whether to accept reparations from Germany', Center for Israel Education, https://israeled.org/resources/documents/menachem-begin-on-whether-to-accept-reparations-from-germany/.
13 'Textiles (In Israel)', Jewish Virtual Library, 2008, https://www.jewishvirtuallibrary.org/textiles.
14 *Australian Jewish News*, 6 November 1959.
15 Fink Family private papers.
16 *Australian Jewish News*, June 1960.
17 Taft and Markus, *A Second Chance*, 269.
18 Hanna Yablonka, *The State of Israel vs Adolf Eichmann* (New York: Schocken Books, 2004).

19   'Ashdod, Israel', New World Encyclopedia, 2016, https://www. newworldencyclopedia.org/entry/Ashdod,_Israel.

20   Ibid.

21   Fink Family private papers.

22   'Mr Rogosin and the Israel Economy', *The Canadian Jewish Chronicle*, 10 April 1958.

23   *The Jerusalem Post*, 15 May 1963.

24   *Australian Jewish News*, 28 August 1987.

25   Fink Family private papers.

26   Fink Family private papers.

27   Fink Family private papers.

28   Fink Family private papers.

29   Fink Family private papers.

30   Fink Family private papers.

31   *Australian Jewish News*, 28 August 1987.

32   Fink Family private papers.

33   Fink Family private papers.

34   Fink Family private papers.

35   Fink Family private papers.

36   Fink Family private papers.

37   *Australian Jewish News*, 29 September 1972.

38   Fink Family private papers.

39   Fink Family private papers.

Chapter 10: Being Mina

1   *Australian Jewish News*, 11 September 1987.

2   *Courier Mail*, 16 June 1970.

3   Newton, *Making a Difference*, 49.

4   Newton, *Making a Difference*, 37.

5   *Council Bulletin*, August 1967.

6   Shirleene Robinson and Julie Ustinoff, eds. *The 1960s in Australia: People, Power and Politics* (Newcastle upon Tyne: Cambridge Scholars Publishing, 2012).

7   Cairo Radio, 22 and 27 May 1967.

8   *Council Bulletin*, August 1967.

9   *Canberra Times*, 24 May 1967.

10   'Women's rights movement', Britannica, 2020, https://www.britannica.com/ event/womens-movement.

11   *Courier Mail*, 16 June 1970.

12   'Gender Equality Milestones', Victorian Women's Trust, 2020, https:// www.vwt.org.au/gender-equality-timeline-australia/.

13 Newton, *Making a Difference*, 43.
14 Newton, *Making a Difference*, 30.
15 *Council Bulletin*, 4 September 1990.
16 Letter 20 June 1976, Fink Family private papers.
17 Malvina Malinek, *Talking Histories*, 11 December 2002.
18 Newton, *Making a Difference*, 238.
19 *Australian Jewish News*, 26 September 1969.
20 *Courier Mail*, 16 June 1970.
21 *Courier Mail*, 16 June 1970.
22 *Courier Mail*, 16 June 1970.
23 'Women who worked for women's causes', *Woman's Day*, 8 December 1975.
24 NCJW Board meeting minutes, 27 May 1980.
25 *Australian Jewish Times*, 20 June 1975.
26 NCJW Board meeting minutes, 27 May 1980.
27 'Matching the deed to the need', NCJW Conference proceedings, Surfers Paradise, 1982.
28 *Council Bulletin*, 3 September 1985.
29 Fink Family private papers.
30 'About ANU – Museum of the Jewish People', Museum of the Jewish People, 2020, https://www.bh.org.il/about-us/about-beit-hatfutsot/.
31 Australian Friends of the Hebrew University of Jerusalem, 'The Golda Meir Fellowship for Post-Doctoral Research', 2015, https://austfhu.org.au/students/admissions/scholarship-opportunities/golda-meir-fellowship/.
32 Nathan Fink, *Talking Histories*, 11 December 2002.
33 Andrew Markus and Margaret Taft eds., *Walter Lippmann, Ethnic Communities Leader: 'Creative Thinker, Dogged Worker, The Kindest of Men'* (Melbourne: Australian Centre for Jewish Civilisation, Monash University, 2016).
34 *Australian Jewish News*, 24 September 1976.
35 *Australian Jewish News*, 15 October 1976.
36 Fink Family private papers.
37 *Australian Jewish News*, 4 September 1987.
38 *Australian Jewish News*, 4 September 1987.

Chapter 11: Back to the Holocaust

1 *The Sun*, 16 February 1983; *The Age*, 23 February 1983.
2 Sheva Glas-Wiener, *Children of the Ghetto* (Melbourne: Globe Press, 1983).
3 Ibid.
4 Lucjan Dobroszycki ed., *The Chronicle of the Lodz Ghetto 1941–1944* (New Haven: Yale University Press, 1994), xxv.
5 Isaiah Trunk, *Lodz Ghetto*, trans. Robert Shapiro (Bloomington: Indiana University Press, 2008).

6   *The Age*, 23 February 1983.

7   'Rumkowski's Address at the Time of the Deportation of the Children of the Lodz Ghetto, September 4, 1942'. Shoah Resource Center, https://www.yadvashem.org/odot_pdf/Microsoft%20Word%20-%205375.pdf.

8   Patrick Montague, *Chełmno and the Holocaust: The History of Hitler's First Death Camp* (Chapel Hill: The University of North Carolina Press, 2012).

9   *The Australian*, 5 March 1983.

10 Fink Family private papers.

11 Fink Family private papers.

12 *Australian Jewish News*, 11 March 1983.

13 *The Age*, 24 May 1983.

14 *The Australian Jewish Times*, 27 October 1983.

15 Fink Family private papers.

16 Deborah Lipstadt, *Denying the Holocaust: The Growing Assault on Truth and Memory* (New York: Penguin Books, 1994); Michael Shermer and Alex Grobman, *Denying History* (Los Angeles: University of California Press, 2009).

17 Margaret Taft, *From Victim to Survivor: The Emergence and Development of the Holocaust Witness 1941–1949* (London, Vallentine Mitchell, 2013), 121.

18 Ibid.

19 Taft and Markus, *A Second Chance*, 188–190.

20 Steven Cooke and Donna-Lee Frieze, *The Interior of our Memories: A History of Melbourne's Jewish Holocaust Centre* (Melbourne: Hybrid Publishers, 2015), 26.

21 Cooke and Frieze, *The Interior of our Memories*, 27.

22 Jewish Holocaust Centre pamphlet, 4 March 1984.

23 Jewish Holocaust Centre Board minutes, 6 March 1984 and 3 May 1984.

24 Jewish Holocaust Centre Board minutes, 23 October 1986.

25 Jewish Holocaust Centre newsletter covering activities for 1985.

26 Jewish Holocaust Centre newsletter covering activities for 1985.

27 Jewish Holocaust Centre newsletter covering activities for 1985.

28 Cooke and Frieze, *The Interior of our Memories*, 152.

29 Saba Feniger, *Talking Histories*, 11 December 2002.

30 Cooke and Frieze, *The Interior of our Memories*, 197.

31 Lillian Tell, *Shloshim Evening for Mina Fink* (reprinted in *Kew Hebrew Congregation Newsletter*, September 1990).

32 Fink Family private papers.

33 Nathan Fink, *Talking Histories*, 11 December 2002.

34 Fink, *Talking Histories*.

35 Lillian Tell, *Shloshim Evening for Mina Fink* (reprinted in *Kew Hebrew Congregation Newsletter*, September 1990).

36 Fink, *Talking Histories*.

Legacy

1 *United Jewish Overseas Relief Fund 1943–44 Annual Report.*
2 *Australian Jewish News*, 1 October 1976.
3 Fink Family private papers.
4 Fink Family private papers.
5 Sermon held in Fink family private papers.
6 Speech held in Fink family private papers.
7 *Kew Hebrew Congregation Newsletter*, September 1990.

BIBLIOGRAPHY

Newspapers
Australian Jewish Herald
Australian Jewish News
Australian Jewish Times
Barrier Miner
Canberra Times
Courier Mail
Daily Telegraph
Hebrew Standard of Australasia
Melbourne Herald
Morning Bulletin
Newcastle Morning Herald
Singleton Argus
Sydney Jewish News
Sydney Morning Herald
The Age
The Argus
The Australian
The Australian Jewish Times
The Canadian Jewish Chronicle
The Jerusalem Post
The Kalgoorlie Miner
The Sun

Reports, Minutes, Magazines
Kadimah Annual Report 1942.
JPRF Board of Management meeting minutes, 20 June 1943.
JPRF Executive meeting minutes, 7 July 1943.
UJORF Annual General Meeting Report, 30 June 1944.
UJORF Annual General Meeting Report, 30 June 1945.
UJRF and UJORF Executive meeting minutes.
UJRF and UJORF Board meeting minutes.
Victory Year 1945: The Story of Melbourne Jewry's Contribution to Overseas Relief, UJORF June 1945.
UJORF Executive Board meeting minutes, 8 July 1946.
UJORF Executive Board meeting minutes, 26 February 1946.

AJWS Directors meeting minutes, 5 August 1946.

UJORF Board meeting minutes, 2 December 1947.

A Record of the Activities of the Australian Jewish Welfare and Relief Society from 1943–1953.

AJWRS Annual Report 1947–48.

Minutes of meeting between AJWRS Executive and Emery Komlos, 8 September 1949.

AJWRS Board meeting minutes 1 November 1948.

Australian Jewish Welfare and Relief Society report 1953.

NCJW Council Bulletin, June/July 1957.

Jewish Holocaust Centre Board minutes, 24 March 1983 – 13 November 1987.

'Women who worked for women's causes', *Woman's Day*, 8 December 1975.

'Matching the deed to the need', NCJW Conference proceedings, Surfers Paradise, 1982.

Jewish Holocaust Centre pamphlet, 4 March 1984.

Jewish Holocaust Centre newsletter covering activities for 1985.

Council Bulletin, 3 September 1985.

'Leo Fink – A Tribute', *Centre News*, June 1987.

Welcare, September 1987.

Archives, Surveys

Leo and Mina Fink Papers, University of Melbourne Archives, 1990.0091.

Fink Family private papers.

Emery Komlos, 'Survey of Jewish Migration and Settlement in Australia', 26 October 1949, file 438, France IV, HIAS-HICEM-NY.

Interviews, Public Addresses

Lillian Tell, *Shloshim Evening for Mina Fink* (reprinted in *Kew Hebrew Congregation Newsletter*, September 1990).

Malvina Malinek. *Talking Histories: Mina Fink*, 11 December 2002.

Nathan Fink, *Talking Histories: Mina Fink*, 11 December 2002.

Saba Feniger, *Talking Histories: Mina Fink*, 11 December 2002.

Max Zilberman, *Talking Histories: Mina Fink*, 11 December 2002.

Nathan Fink, interview by Margaret Taft (East Melbourne, Victoria, 27 November 2018).

Freda Freiberg, interview by Margaret Taft (South Yarra, Victoria, 13 December 2018).

Barry Fink and Leon Fink, interview by Margaret Taft (Toorak, Victoria, 23 February 2019).

Colin Golvan, interview by Margaret Taft (Southbank, Victoria, 26 June 2019).

Secondary Sources

Ajzenbud, Moshe. *60 Years of 'Bund' in Melbourne 1928–1988*. Melbourne: Jewish Labour Bund, 1996.

Allon, Fiona. 'At home in the Suburbs'. *History Australia* 11, no. 1 (2014).

Aly, Götz. *Europe Against the Jews, 1880–1945*. New York: Metropolitan Books, 2020.

Beaumont, Joan ed. *Australia's War, 1939–45*. Crows Nest: Allen & Unwin, 1996.

Ben-Arieh, Yehoshua. *The Making of Eretz Israel in the Modern Era*. Jerusalem: Hebrew University Magnes Press, 2018.

Benjamin, Rodney. *'A Serious Influx of Jews' A History of Jewish Welfare in Victoria*. St Leonards, NSW: Allen & Unwin, 1998.

Blainey, Geoffrey. *A History of Victoria*. Melbourne: Cambridge University Press, 2013.

Brett, Judith. *Robert Menzies' Forgotten People*. Carlton: Melbourne University Press, 2007.

Brodsky, Alexandra Fanny. *In Pursuit of a Dream; A Time in Australia*. London & NY: The Radcliffe Press, 2007.

Browning, Christopher. *The Path to Genocide: Essays on Launching the Final Solution*, Cambridge: Cambridge University Press, 1992.

Cooke, Steven, and Donna-Lee Frieze. *The Interior of our Memories: A History of Melbourne's Jewish Holocaust Centre*. Melbourne: Hybrid Publishers, 2015.

Cooper, Leo. *In the Shadow of the Polish Eagle: The Poles, the Holocaust and Beyond*. London: Palgrave, 2000.

Dapin, Mark. *Jewish Anzacs: Jews in the Australian Military*. Sydney: New South Publishing, 2017.

Darian-Smith, Kate. *On the Home Front; Melbourne in Wartime: 1939–1945*. Melbourne: Melbourne University Press, 2009 (1990).

Dingle, Tony, and Seamus O'Hanlon. 'Modernism versus domesticity: The contest to shape Melbourne's homes, 1945–1969'. *Australian Historical Studies* 27 (1997).

Dobroszycki, Lucjan ed. *The Chronicle of the Lodz Ghetto 1941–1944*. New Haven: Yale University Press, 1994.

Eisenstein, Miriam. *Jewish Schools in Poland 1919–39: Their Philosophy and Development*. New York, Columbia Press, 1950.

Fishman, David E. *The Rise of Modern Yiddish Culture*. Pittsburgh: University of Pittsburgh Press, 2005.

Fitzpatrick, Peter. *After 'the Doll': Australian Drama Since 1955*. Melbourne: Edward Arnold (Australia), 1979.

Freeze, ChaeRan, Paula Hyman, and Antony Polonsky, eds. *Polin: Studies in Polish Jewry Volume 18: Jewish Women in Eastern Europe*. Portland, OR: The Littman Library of Jewish Civilization, 2007.

Glas-Wiener, Sheva. *Children of the Ghetto*. Melbourne: Globe Press, 1983.

Gilbert, Martin. *Israel A History*. London: Doubleday, 1998.

Gilbert, Martin. *Routledge Atlas of the Holocaust*. London: Routledge, 2002.

Golvan, Colin. *The Distant Exodus*. Crows Nest, NSW: ABC Enterprises, 1990.

Heller, Celia S. *On the Edge of Destruction: Jews of Poland Between the Two World Wars*. Detroit: Wayne University Press, 1977.

Hitchins, Keith. *Rumania, 1866–1947*. Oxford: Oxford University Press, 1994.

Hyman, Paula. 'Eastern European Jewish Women in an Age of Transition, 1880–1930'. In *Jewish Women in Historical Perspective,* edited by Judith Baskin. Detroit: Wayne State University Press, 1998.

Jona, Walter. 'The VAJEX Story: Achievements in War and Peace'. *Australian Jewish Historical Society Journal* XII, no. 1 (1993).

Kobrin, Rebecca. *Jewish Bialystok and Its Diaspora*. Bloomington: Indiana University Press, 2010.

Laqueur, Walter. *History of Zionism*. New York: Schocken Books, 1989.

Liberman, Serge. 'Seventy Years of Yiddish Theatre in Melbourne (1909–1979)'. Part 2, *Melbourne Chronicle,* January 1981.

Lipstadt Deborah. *Denying the Holocaust: The Growing Assault on Truth and Memory*. New York: Penguin Books, 1994.

MacLean, Pam. 'Jewish Migration in the Twenties: A Jewish Pioneering Tradition in Australia?' *Meanjin* 42, no. 1 (March 1983).

Madigan, Edward, and Gideon Reuveni, eds. *The Jewish Experience of the First World War*. London: Palgrave Macmillan, 2019.

Mandel, Daniel. 'A Good International Citizen: H.V. Evatt, Britain, the United Nations and Israel, 1948–49'. *Middle Eastern Studies* 39, no. 2 (April 2003).

Mann, Klaus. *The Turning Point: Thirty-five Years in this Century, the Autobiography of Klaus Mann*. Lexington: Plunkett Lake Press, 2017 (c.1942).

Markus, Andrew, and Margaret Taft, eds. *Walter Lippmann, Ethnic Communities Leader: 'Creative Thinker, Dogged Worker, The Kindest of Men'*. Melbourne: Australian Centre for Jewish Civilisation, Monash University, 2016.

McKernan, Michael. *All In! Australia During the Second World War*. Melbourne: Thomas Nelson Australia, 1983.

Montague, Patrick. *Chełmno and the Holocaust: The History of Hitler's First Death Camp*. Chapel Hill: The University of North Carolina Press, 2012.

Murphy, John. *Imagining the Fifties*. Sydney: UNSW Press, 2000.

Near, Henry. *The Kibbutz Movement: A History, Origins and Growth 1909–1939*, Vol. 1. Oxford: Oxford University Press, 1992.

Newton, Marlo. *Making a Difference: A History of the National Council of Jewish Women*. Melbourne: Hybrid Publishers, 2000.

Neumann, Klaus. *Across the Seas: Australia's Response to Refugees, a History*. Melbourne: Black Inc., 2015.

Oeser, O.A., and S.B. Hammond. *Social Structure and Personality in a City*. London: Routledge, 1954.

O'Hanlon, Seamus. 'Hostels for Migrant Workers in Early Postwar Melbourne'. *History Australia* 2, no. 3 (2005).

Pierce, Peter. *The Cambridge History of Australian Literature*. Melbourne: Cambridge University Press, 2011.

Plowman, Peter. *Australian Migrant Ships 1946–77*. Sydney: Rosenberg Publishing, 2006.

Price, Charles A. 'Jewish Settlers in Australia'. *Australian Jewish Historical Society Journal and Proceedings*, V, Part 8 (1964).

Richardson, Nick. *1956: The Year Australia Welcomed the World*. Melbourne: Scribe Publications, 2019.

Robinson, Shirleene, and Julie Ustinoff, eds. *The 1960s in Australia: People, Power and Politics*. Newcastle upon Tyne: Cambridge Scholars Publishing, 2012.

Rogers, Dorothy. *A History of Kew*. Melbourne: Lowden Publishing Company, 1973.

Ro'l, Yaacov, ed. *Jews and Jewish life in Russia and the Soviet Union*. Essex: Frank Cass & Co. Ltd., 2016.

Rubinstein, Colin, and Tzvi Fleischer. 'A distant affinity: The History of Australian-Israeli Relations'. *Jewish Political Studies Review* 19, no. 3/4 (Fall 2007).

Rubinstein, Hilary. *The Jews in Australia, A Thematic History, Volume 1, 1788–1945*. Melbourne: William Heinemann Australia, 1991.

Rubinstein, WD. *The Jews in Australia: A Thematic History, Volume 2: 1945 to the Present*. Melbourne: William Heinemann Australia, 1991.

Rutland, Suzanne D. '"I Never Knew A Man Who Had So Many Cousins": Differing Attitudes to Postwar Survivor Migration: Melbourne and Sydney'. *Australian Jewish Historical Society Journal* XII, no. 2 (1994).

Rutland, Suzanne D. 'Post war Anti-Jewish Refugee Hysteria: A case of Racial or Religious bigotry?' *Journal of Australian Studies* 27, no. 77 (2003).

Rutland, Suzanne D. *Edge of the Diaspora: Two Centuries of Jewish Settlement in Australia*. Sydney: Brandl & Schlesinger Pty Ltd, 1997.

Rutland, Suzanne D. 'Resettling Survivors of the Holocaust in Australia'. *Holocaust Studies: A Journal of Culture and History* 16, no. 3 (2010).

Rutland, Suzanne D. and Sol Encel. 'Three Rich Uncles in America'. *American Jewish History* 95, no. 1 (2009).

Sachar, Howard *A History of Israel: From the Rise of Zionism to Our Times*. New York: Alfred A Knopf, 1996 (1979).

Sacks, Adam. 'Ostbahnhof Berlin'. *Polin Studies* 32 (2020).

Schneer, Jonathan. *The Balfour Declaration*. London: Bloomsbury Publishing, 2010.

Shermer, Michael, and Alex Grobman. *Denying History*. Los Angeles: University of California Press, 2009.

Sohn, David, ed. *Byalistok bilder album fun a barimter shtot un yire yiden yiber der welt. [Białystok Photo Album of a Renowned City and its Jews the World Over.]* New York: Bialystoker Center, 1951.

Taft, Margaret, and Andrew Markus. *A Second Chance, The Making of Yiddish Melbourne*. Melbourne: Monash University Publishing, 2018.

Taft, Margaret. *From Victim to Survivor: The Emergence and Development of the Holocaust Witness 1941–1949*. London: Vallentine Mitchell, 2013.

Trunk, Isaiah. *Lodz Ghetto, A History*. Translated and edited by Robert Shapiro. Bloomington: Indiana University Press, 2008.

Wasserstein, Bernard. *On the Eve: The Jews of Europe Before the Second World War*. New York: Simon & Schuster, 2012.

Weitz, Eric D. 'Weimar Germany and its Histories'. *Central European Histories* 43, no. 4 (2010).

Wolf-Monzon, Tamar. 'Uri Zvi Greenberg and the pioneers of the Third Aliyah: A Case of Reception'. *Prooftexts* 29, no. 1 (2009).

Yablonka, Hanna. *The State of Israel vs Adolf Eichmann*. New York: Schocken Books, 2004.

Zable, Arnold. *Wanderers and Dreamers: Tales of the David Herman Theatre*. Melbourne: Hyland Press, 1998.

Websites

Abramson, Henry. 'Russian Civil War'. The YIVO Encyclopedia of Jews in Eastern Europe, 2010. https://yivoencyclopedia.org/article.aspx/Russian_Civil_War.

Australian Friends of the Hebrew University of Jerusalem. 'The Golda Meir Fellowship for Post-Doctoral Research', 2015. https://austfhu.org.au/students/admissions/scholarship-opportunities/golda-meir-fellowship/.

Australian Institute for Disaster Resilience. 'Black Friday Bushfires, 1939'. Australian Disaster Resilience Knowledge Hub. https://knowledge.aidr.org.au/resources/bushfire-black-friday-victoria-1939/.

Australian War Memorial. 'Prime Minister Robert G. Menzies: wartime broadcast'. Memorial Articles, 2019. https://www.awm.gov.au/articles/encyclopedia/prime_ministers/menzies.

Australian War Memorial. 'The Charge of the 4th Light Horse Brigade at Beersheba'. Memorial Articles, 2007. https://www.awm.gov.au/articles/blog/the-charge-of-the-4th-light-horse-brigade-at-beersheba.

Barkai, Zeev. 'Textiles (In Israel)'. Jewish Virtual Library, 2008. https://www.jewishvirtuallibrary.org/textiles.

Burkett, Elinor (primary contributor). 'Women's rights movement'. Britannica, 2020. https://www.britannica.com/event/womens-movement.

Cabaret Berlin. 'Josephine Baker: Goin' Bananas', 2010. https://cabaret.berlin/people/josephine-baker/.

214

Bibliography

Carter, David. 'Judah Leon Waten 1911–1985'. Australian Dictionary of
  Biography, 2012. http://adb.anu.edu.au/biography/waten-judah-leon-14884.
Center for Israel Education. 'Menachem Begin on whether
  to accept reparations from Germany'. Documents and
  Sources. https://israeled.org/resources/documents/
  menachem-begin-on-whether-to-accept-reparations-from-germany/.
Derby Sulzers. 'MS Eridan 1928–1956'. 2011. https://www.derbysulzers.com/
  shiperidan.html.
Festival De Cannes World. 'In competition – feature films JEDDA', 1955. http://
  www.festival-cannes.com/en/archives/ficheFilm/id/3702/year/1955.html.
Herșcovici, Lucian-Zeev. 'Galați'. The YIVO Encyclopedia of Jews in Eastern
  Europe, 2010. https://yivoencyclopedia.org/article.aspx/Galati.
Internet Archive. 'Palestine Census (1922)', 2015. https://archive.org/details/
  PalestineCensus1922.
Jewish Virtual Library. 'Fact Sheet: Jewish Refugees from Arab Countries'.
  https://www.jewishvirtuallibrary.org/jewish-refugees-from-arab-countries.
Jewish Virtual Library. 'Galati'. Encyclopedia Judaica, 2008. https://www.
  jewishvirtuallibrary.org/galati.
Jewish Virtual Library. 'Israel's International Relations: Cooperation with Africa',
  2021. https://www.jewishvirtuallibrary.org/israeli-cooperation-with-africa.
Jewish Virtual Library. 'Israeli Population Statistics (1960–2008)', 2008. https://
  www.jewishvirtuallibrary.org/israeli-population-statistics-1960-2008.
Jewish Virtual Library. 'Rosh Pina'. https://www.jewishvirtuallibrary.org/rosh-pina.
Jupp, James cited in Huxley, John. 'When the Boat Came In'. The Age, 2007.
  https://www.theage.com.au/national/when-the-boat-came-in-20070311-
  ge4e9h.html.
Kobrin, Rebecca. 'Białystok'. The YIVO Encyclopedia of Jews in Eastern Europe,
  2010. https://yivoencyclopedia.org/article.aspx/Bialystok.
Museum of the Jewish People. 'About ANU – Museum of the Jewish People',
  2020. https://www.bh.org.il/about-us/about-beit-hatfutsot/.
New World Encyclopedia contributors. 'Ashdod, Israel'. New World Encyclopedia,
  2016. https://www.newworldencyclopedia.org/entry/Ashdod,_Israel.
Sadetsky-Kimron, Ayana. 'Galați, Romania'. JewishGen KehilaLinks, 2008.
  https://kehilalinks.jewishgen.org/galati/galatz_history.htm.
Serle, Geoffrey. 'Sir John Monash 1865–1931'. Australian Dictionary of Biography,
  1986. http://adb.anu.edu.au/biography/monash-sir-john-7618.
South Australian Maritime Museum. 'Citta di Genova'. Passengers in History.
  https://passengers.history.sa.gov.au/node/922955.
Sturma, Michael. 'John Michael O'Keefe 1935–1978'. Australian
  Dictionary of Biography, 2000. http://adb.anu.edu.au/biography/
  okeefe-john-michael-johnny-11293.

United States Holocaust Memorial Museum. 'The Weimar Republic'. Holocaust Encyclopedia. https://encyclopedia.ushmm.org/content/en/article/the-weimar-republic.

Variety. 'On the Beach'. Film Review, 1958. https://variety.com/1958/film/reviews/on-the-beach-1200419354/.

Victorian Women's Trust. 'Gender Equality Milestones', 2020. https://www.vwt.org.au/gender-equality-timeline-australia/.

Yad Vashem. 'Rumkowski's Address at the Time of the Deportation of the Children of the Lodz Ghetto, September 4, 1942'. Shoah Resource Center. https://www.yadvashem.org/odot_pdf/Microsoft%20Word%20-%205375.pdf.

Zalewska, Gabriela. 'Zamenhof, Ludwik'. The YIVO Encyclopedia of Jews in Eastern Europe, 2010. https://yivoencyclopedia.org/article.aspx/Zamenhof_Ludwik.

INDEX

Leo and Mina Fink

  Bialystok 19
  Melbourne 62, 115, 173
Newsweek (magazine) 133
Nigeria 133
Niland, D'Arcy 115
Nissim, Rabbi (Israel) 161
Nobel Peace Prize 179–80
Northcote (Melb) 116
Norway 132
Nosferatu (film, 1922) 36
NSDAP *See* National Socialist German Workers' Party (NSDAP)
Nudel, Ida 162

October revolution *See* Bolshevik revolution
Oeuvre de Secours aux Enfants (Children's Aid Society) 120
Office of Equal Opportunity Commissioner (Vic) 157
O'Keefe, Johnny 114–15
Olympic Games (1956) 123
On the Beach (novel 1957/film) 115
Operation Ezra and Nehemiah 135
Operation Magic Carpet 135
Orama (ship) 51, 54
ORT-OZE (overseas Jewish relief organisation) 63
OSE Central Board (Geneva) 100

Pacific war
  Darwin, bombing of 69
  Singapore, fall of 69
Palestine
  Balfour Declaration 31–32
  British conquest (1916–17) 133
  British Mandate *See* Mandatory Palestine
  Palestinian Liberation Organization 133

UN Partition Plan 132, 133, 134
War of Independence (1948) 96, 142
Palestinian Liberation Organization 133
Partisaner March (the Partisan's song) 182
Partisan's song *(Partisaner March)* 182
Patkin, Benzion 150
Peacock, Andrew 163
Peak Council of National Women's Non-Government Organisations (UN) 163
Peck, Gregory 115
Peretz, IL 62
Perkins, Anthony 115
Perth (WA) 78, 115
Petrov spy affair (1954) 117
Pilsudski, Jozef (Marshal) 57
pioneers ('halutzim') 32–33
  Fink, Leo 32, 33, 35, 42, 130, 131, 151, 191
Pitt, Michael 48
PJRF *See* Polish Jewish Relief Fund (PJRF) (Melb)
pogroms 32, 39, 44
  Bialystok 17, 23, 58
  Kishinev 39
  Kristallnacht 59
Poland 3, 16, 32, 38, 51, 52, 62, 89, 132, 144
  Agudah schools 27
  antisemitism 34, 57–59
  Beis Yaacov schools 27, 28
  Bialystok *See* Bialystok (Poland)
  Catholicism 58
  Chelmno (death camp) 172
  death camps 67, 172
  Endecja party 57
  German invasion 66, 171
  Horev schools 27

232

ABOUT THE AUTHOR

Dr Margaret Taft is a research associate at the Australian Centre for Jewish Civilisation at Monash University. For the past 12 years her research has focused on the reconstruction of Jewish immigrant life in pre-war and post-war 20th-century Australia. Her particular interest lies with the Yiddish speakers from Eastern Europe whose personal agency, leadership and cultural identity transformed what had been a predominantly Anglo Jewish community.

Margaret is an experienced author, teacher, lecturer and public speaker. Her publications include *From Victim to Survivor: The Emergence and Development of the Holocaust Witness 1941–1949* and *A Second Chance: The Making of Yiddish Melbourne*, which was shortlisted for the 2019 Victorian Community History Awards. The daughter of Holocaust survivors, her early years were spent in the culturally rich post-war immigrant community of Northcote.